Reconceptualising Disability for the Contemporary Church

Reconceptualising Disability for the Contemporary Church

Frances Mackenney-Jeffs

scm press

© Frances Mackenney-Jeffs 2021

Published in 2021 by SCM Press
Editorial office
3rd Floor, Invicta House,
108–114 Golden Lane,
London EC1Y 0TG, UK
www.scmpress.co.uk

SCM Press is an imprint of Hymns Ancient & Modern Ltd
(a registered charity)

Hymns Ancient & Modern® is a registered trademark of
Hymns Ancient & Modern Ltd
13A Hellesdon Park Road, Norwich,
Norfolk NR6 5DR, UK

British Library Cataloguing in Publication data
A catalogue record for this book is available
from the British Library

978-0-334-05917-2

Typeset by Regent Typesetting

Contents

In gratitude and honour to all the exemplary men who have shaped and are shaping my life: my father Vic, my brother Julian, my husband Andrew and our dear son Sam.

And not forgetting my dear mother who, though believing domestic matters to be of utmost concern, discerned that I had it in me to write on theology and duly anticipated that work.

Acknowledgements

The writing of this book has been part of a much longer and deeper project that started in 2003 at King's College London as a PhD in education research and theology under the supervision of Canon Professor Andrew Walker. My original aim was to write on exclusion in the church, sweeping across race, gender, age and disability. But I needed to narrow down to one factor for the depth of study required of a doctorate. In 2005 my brother died suddenly and then two years later, my mother, due to the appalling distress of losing her son after her husband. Our family went into meltdown and our 12-year-old son, a highly sensitive boy, became very ill. I had already turned towards disability as my area of study. I had no idea how my own personal trajectory was to become so much a part of this research project. I wish to thank Andrew Walker for his pastoral sensitivity and wisdom in moving me away from an exclusive focus on gender and in leading me to spend the first year after my brother's death reading on the theology of suffering, which began to equip me to see with different eyes the world I had entered by force. In time Andrew had to bow out on health grounds, and I thank Professor Andrew Wright for taking me on, and for bringing so much shape to my work at this stage. I thank them both for their grace towards me at a very unstable time in my life where the completion of a PhD was particularly daunting.

I also wish to thank the Revd Peter Levell from my former church, who was once the CEO of Causeway Prospects, the charity for people with learning disabilities. His passion for inclusion of people with learning disabilities led him to visit me on a regular basis to pray with me for my work. His kindness and encouragement were greatly appreciated at a very depleted time.

For the sake of anonymity, I haven't named the many people who were part of the research work at the core of this book. For those who know who they are I give my profound thanks for their grace towards me in what might have been perplexing for them at times.

And now to the final Andrew, my devoted husband, who shouldered so much of the task of our life as a family in order for me to pursue what he believed was my calling.

And, last but not least, to Sam who was swept away by the trauma in the family and became a major player in this work as we were led to reconsider what being a human being means when it is no longer possible to jump through all the hoops that our success culture demands.

Introduction

Context

Disability in the twenty-first century is a topic that has come of age. There is a view that it is the last civil rights movement (Driedger 1989), coming as it does after a degree of liberation for women, black, Asian and minority ethnic and LGBTQ+ people. Predictably, perhaps, now that society has turned its attention to disability as a form of social oppression, the church has been taking stock of the fact and considering its own position on the subject. My doctoral work (which this book draws on) sought to uncover the extent to which disability is negatively constructed in the Christian church and the degree to which the church is exclusive, and/or oppressive, of disabled people in its practices. Furthermore, it sought to consolidate some of the progress made as a result of disability legislation in the US and Britain, and the high profile that legal requirements accorded the matter in the conviction that there was something of a *kairos* moment here (probably initiated by the Holy Spirit) for people with disabilities in the church. While this was my starting point, as I journeyed in my own personal circumstances and on the project of this book I came to see disability as a lens through which the church can see itself more clearly and embrace the countercultural call of the gospel to extend the loving welcome of Christ to all those commonly rejected in wider society and often by the institutional church. So this book is more a call to the church to be all that God intends rather than a tokenist attempt at inclusion of people with disabilities.

While society is of interest, there is a specific focus here on the Christian church, and particularly on its Evangelical sector. Evangelicalism was selected as I have most experience of this approach and anticipated that it might have difficulty with offering full inclusion to persons with intellectual disabilities because of its bias towards the rational and concern with 'good order'.

There are four main areas of disability: physical impairments, sensory impairments, learning disabilities and mental health needs. Learning disability is the politically correct replacement for 'mental retardation', which is a term still in current use in the United States but not in Britain. Learning disability is synonymous with intellectual impairment. Previously, learning disability was subsumed under mental health needs but the two categories are seen as totally distinct now. However, because of this historical tendency, in the literature the two may be conflated. This book focuses on the first three areas: physical impairments, sensory impairments and learning disabilities, giving priority to factors that are visible and permanent as the likely causes of a person being persistently marginalized within mainstream culture. Of the three, particular focus is placed on intellectual impairment. The empirical work was conducted with this constituency as it was thought that if those with learning disabilities were fully included then all others were likely to be too; for intellectual disability had been a late addition to the field.

The attempt to unify all people with impairments has not been unproblematic. From the 1960s organizations were formed that crossed impairment boundaries, the BCODP (British Council of Organisations of Disabled People) being one formed in the 1980s. Despite the need for solidarity, disabled people often internalize society's attitudes regarding disability, and wish to distance themselves from others with dissimilar impairments which may be perceived as worse than their own (French 1993, p. 22). Thus a wheelchair user with spinal cord injury may not really consider themselves comparable with someone who is intellectually disabled (Oliver 1993). Thus the intellectually disabled became a marginalized group within disability itself (Leach 1991; Aspis 1991; Walmsley 1993).

Author Location

My passion for inclusion undoubtedly comes from my own experience of exclusion in some sectors of the church. Many of my early years as a Christian were spent in the ultra-conservative Restoration Movement which came out of the Brethren Church. It is my contention that while they parted company over the gifts of the Spirit in the church today, the Restoration Movement uncritically retained the Brethren Church's worldview regarding gender, which it had subconsciously absorbed. Being a mature, single woman at that time I was further disadvantaged because women were only truly valued through marriage. The Restoration Movement did not actively teach an Augustinian view of women, but its teaching was consonant with that. In *Misogyny and the Western Philosophical Tradition*, Beverly Clack summarizes Augustine's view of the imago Dei: 'man is completely in the image of God whereas woman is only in the image of the divine when in partnership with her husband' (Clack 1999, p. 63).

From this very negative and prolonged experience I developed a passion for inclusivity not least because while the church may be excluding, the gospel is clearly not. I listened to those involved in the secular Disability Movement, and their criticisms of the church resonated with my own experience. Yet my understanding of the gospel was at odds with my life experience, and I seriously wanted the church to be true to her calling to be the Body of Christ on earth, drawing rather than repelling broken people and causing further damage. I also use some feminist sources because after my 'wilderness' decade in the ultra-conservative church I found the emancipatory writings of some feminists and especially some Christian feminists to be a source of strength and hope.

Up to this point I cannot claim any great passion or even concern for people with intellectual impairments. When I was about to embark on some research with people with intellectual disabilities, I felt deeply challenged by whether I really cared about full inclusion for *all* people, or just cared about people like me. This led to some deep soul searching, but I found that despite the fear of involvement with people with intellectual impairments en masse (a reality that even Frances Young admitted to early on (1990, p. 100)), deep down I did care desperately for the fairness of the gospel to be made manifest. I also thought that if people with profound intellectual disabilities were included then it probably meant that no one else would be excluded.

My conversation partners are drawn from the secular world, because I believed it was important to listen to the Disability Rights Movement, also called the Disability Movement. It is an international group of organizations working together for equal opportunities and accessibility for people with disability (see definition on page 25). I have also drawn on a range of writers from different theological stables, thus making the Christian side of the work ecumenical yet thoroughly orthodox. Christian writers such as Stanley Hauerwas, Mary Grey, Serene Jones, Jean Vanier, Letty Russell and John Swinton have in common a healthy disregard for the status quo and its tendency to be elitist, and thus against the grain of the gospel.

Although I am a committed Christian this should not imply that I am uncritical of the church and particularly of its practices when it comes to issues of social inclusion. Although I value the Evangelical church for introducing me to Jesus, and the charismatic movement for teaching me about the gifts of the Holy Spirit, there is much that can be learned from other Christian traditions. I would also like to add that I am grateful for the many loving relationships that I formed while in Restoration, many of which still endure. We are all a mix of light and shade, and the churches we form are similarly an expression of that. Although I am writing as a Christian feminist, my beliefs and faith commitments are thoroughly orthodox: I hold to classical incarnational Christianity and am working ecumenically here with Catholic, Orthodox, Presbyterian, Pentecostal and Evangelical theologians. To those readers for whom the word 'feminist' is a term of opprobrium: a word of explanation. In ultra-conservative circles the term serves as a form of branding in a similar way that Communism did in the McCarthy era in the US. For this reason I am reluctant to use the term. However, the life of Jesus was emancipating for all the women he met and there are those who would claim that Jesus was a feminist! At one time anyone who thought women should have the vote and an education would have counted as feminist. Alan Alda in the television series *Mash* says that a feminist is anyone who thinks women are human beings too. I do not conflate 'Girl Power' – which is basically women behaving as badly as men sometimes do – with feminism, which actually has Christian origins, becoming a global movement out of the Christian Women's Temperance Movement in America in the nineteenth century. For those who wish to know more about this I refer the reader to Elaine Storkey's *What's Right with Feminism* (1985), or to Serene Jones' more theological *Feminist Theory and Christian Theology* (2000).

Outline

This book comprises eight chapters, apart from the Introduction and Conclusion. Its aim is to equip clergy and the many lay people who engage in ministry with disabled people to think more deeply about the relationship between the church and disabled people and to be mindful of the dangers that lie in that direction. Chapter 1 sets out the historical perspective on disability from a mostly western worldview. This is in order to show that disability is a cultural construct and not universal. Ancient civilizations of the Near East are briefly examined and reveal a surprising level of inclusion of people with impairments, for 'disabled' people were not yet a marked group on the edge of society, but were fully integrated into the rural life of the community. The Classical world is then explored for its particular relevance to western civilization, for the Ancient Greeks laid its foundations. The bias and culture of the Ancient Greeks are set out as we discover that they are embedded in our own societal assumptions. Among these are the concept of stigma, bodily and intellectual fitness, and a high regard for physical perfection; and the associated infanticide of babies born with impairments. In Sparta it was a legal requirement to expose infants to the elements and withdraw any duty of care. Another extreme tendency was attributed to Cicero who regarded disabled and deformed people as good material for mockery and general entertainment.

The Medieval era is explored next. Here again we see the easy accommodation of disabled people in the rural life of the community. The 'village idiot' was a much-loved character who fulfilled a legitimate social role which later disappeared. The point to notice is that disabled individuals were known as persons and not yet objectified. Finkelstein (1980, 1981) claims that a major shift occurred after the Industrial Revolution, where mechanization was introduced for a standard user, thus excluding many disabled people.

From here we move into an exploration of 'Medieval synthesis', the melding of Greek philosophy with Judaeo-Christian thought. Augustine and Thomas Aquinas are the main players here and it could be argued it was at this point that much of the emancipatory thrust of the gospel was submerged under Greek philosophy. In order to recover the purity of the gospel in regard to full inclusion of disabled persons we need to acknowledge this development.

Judaeo-Christian perspectives are examined next, as the Disability Movement lays some strong charges against this worldview. The movement could be said to have hampered itself with a wrong reading of Judaeo-Christian theology, especially as Jewish psychologist Ellen Wertlieb points out that many Jewish heroes of faith were themselves disabled. Wertlieb tests the claims, even assumptions of the Disability Movement, and offers some very unexpected conclusions. From here we move on to examine the historical Jesus with regard to disability issues. We engage with some of the critics of the historical Jesus from the Disability Movement who feel the miracles make them 'disappear'. We also note an anachronistic overlay on the first century of modern frameworks creating a problem that was not there in the original context.

We then pick up with the sixteenth century and explore up to and including the Victorian era. The eighteenth and nineteenth centuries are noted as becoming more oppressive to

disabled people on account of prevailing ideologies, in particular the new 'scientific' worldview. Some measures regarding
education were oppressive, as parents were obliged to send
their disabled children to the appropriate school regardless
of its geographical location. Also in this period people with
cognitive impairments and/or learning disabilities were categorized as the same as those with mental illness, and this group
was also denied the right of choice over where they lived. Colin
Barnes in *Disabled People in Britain and Discrimination* notes
that the dominance of the medical profession in all aspects of
disability dates back to this time.

Moving on to the modern era we note the fallout from
two world wars, including the many war wounded vying
for the same resources as those with impairments. In 1948
welfare-based services were introduced, which led to disability
becoming a social category in order for full provision to be
made. The intention was positive, but the unintended consequence was that disabled people became a marked group on
the edge of society.

Coming full circle to end with recent attitudes, we note some
positive moves from the 1970s onwards, as disabled people
started to insist on self-representation. In the 1990s disability
became highly politicized by some disabled academics who gave
it a sociological rationale. Some writers lament the politicizing
of disability but there is truth in the saying that 'the personal is
political'. A hierarchy of disability became evident, with intellectual wheelchair users such as the first professor of disability
studies, Mike Oliver, to the fore, which caused intellectual disability to become the poor relation. However, at the same time
some Christian theologians argued for the centrality of people
with intellectual impairments in the Christian church. The
moral meaning of disability underwent a radical shift as focus
moved from the passive reception of charity to the dignity of
full human rights and participation in the public arena.

In Chapter 2 we explore some vital theoretical models of
disability, with the endemic medical model at one end and the
social model at the other, with a raft of other models that can
be charted somewhere between them. These models undergird

what has become the academic subject of disability studies as a subtopic of sociology. These models are discussed and critiqued, as it is vital that we see how the models impact our own thinking. Many of those working in the church with disabled people have little or no awareness of these models, which they may unknowingly have internalized. Some models of disability are introduced here in order that research with disabled people be conducted in an ethical and rigorous manner. Here I reveal my own difficulties with researching people with intellectual disabilities while trying to follow a *critical disability research* framework. Other, more recent methods are then suggested, and the research work of Swinton, Baines and Mowat from Aberdeen, Jill Harshaw from Belfast, and Melanie Nind from Southampton are introduced.

Chapter 3 continues to engage with some underlying assumptions that need examination. Principally, it explores what being a human being means. Two further models that have a spiritual element are introduced. First, the limits model from Deborah Creamer's *Christian Theology and Disability*. From here 'individual', 'the Self' and 'person' are explored in contrast to each other in order to lay a foundation for a theological exploration of personhood. After establishing that we are full persons as ourselves in Christ, a final model of disability is introduced from the Ukrainian Tataryns, who advocate a Trinitarian model of disability in order to promote a more inclusive and welcoming church culture.

Chapter 4 continues to work towards a more constructive theology of disability in unpacking further elements. The global scene is encountered through the extensive work of Bedirhan et al. for the World Health Organization. This is set out under four main headings relating to disability:

1   Attitudes and beliefs.
2   Stigma.
3   Gender.
4   Personhood.

We recognize here a folkloric belief in the reasons for disability, which sometimes surfaces in the West through popular theology. In order to disempower this toxic force, we explore a robust and thoroughly biblical theology of suffering, which has become out of vogue in the present era of 'happily ever after'. This exploration includes a personal account of my journey that led to this in-depth work on the theology of suffering.

Chapter 5 moves into complex territory as we comprehensively explore fresh theological perspectives that acknowledge the issue of disability. Some difficult terms are encountered, and readers are advised to turn to the Glossary to understand the arguments throughout. I had to familiarize myself with the terms in order to make the arguments. The intention is to bring clarity and encouragement. The beginning of the chapter looks at issues of biblical interpretation and then raises the issue of how to preach constructively for those who deliver homilies. Metaphors are seen to be problematic and here sensory disability is to the fore. The work of Kathy Black, professor of homiletics, the late John Hull, blind professor of education, and Louise Lawrence, biblical scholar, are used here. Some issues relating to deafness are also covered followed by a brief mention of mental illness.

An inclusive ecclesiology is set out, followed by some key disability theologians. Some models of God for disability inclusion are introduced. It is noted that a number of disabled researchers have made use of liberation theology, a movement the DM seems wholly unaware of, despite the fact that critics often regard the two movements as Marxist in flavour. The Pentecostal theologian Amos Yong has pressed for a reformulation of some core Christian doctrines to accommodate the reality of disability, in particular the doctrine of the resurrection body in the eschaton. His argument focuses in particular on people with Downs syndrome and there is a rich debate between Amos Yong and Ryan Mullins (in the online Journal of Religion and Disability, *Ars Disputandi*), both of whom are concerned for the welfare of disabled people and have had a sibling with Downs syndrome. They do not come to the same conclusion, yet inclusion of some points from a philosophical piece by Terrence Ehrman enables us to shed further light on the subject of identity in the hereafter, without having to take sides with Mullins or Yong.

Chapter 6 begins with charting ways in which the church has moved towards greater inclusion. Following this we reflect on some of the criticisms of the DM and then consider some of the tensions between the gospel and the institutional church. We then move on to the contemporary church and look at some refreshing and probably little-known new initiatives for people with intellectual impairments.

Recent initiatives fall into three categories: parachurch ministries such as L'Arche, Causeway Prospects, SPRED and Faith and Light. Then there are two fresh expressions of church which are aimed particularly at people with intellectual impairments. These follow a separatist model in order to accommodate a specific culture. Finally we encounter a fully intergrationist model of church at Fresh Wind Christian Fellowship in British Columbia, Canada, where the power relations are turned upside down. Pastor Brad Jersak refers to a number of people with learning disabilities as the pillars of his church. He has a number of people with Downs syndrome who he calls pastors. The people with learning disabilities in his church use their gifts in specific ways that the congregation has learned to appreciate. For example some people with Downs syndrome who cannot read spend hours poring over the Bible and sometimes areas of significance are highlighted to them by the Holy Spirit which they can point out to others who can read. The significant thing to note here is that people with intellectual impairments are not expected to behave as others but are accepted and welcomed on their own terms.

Chapter 7 uses interview material conducted with parents of offspring with intellectual impairments. From these interviews it is possible to identify which model of disability the parent started out with and any shift that may have occurred. From the writings of Frances Young it is possible to compile a similar interview with her work to see where she sits alongside others. I have included her as she had an enormous paradigm shift some years after the birth of her profoundly disabled son Arthur.

This chapter seeks to show the real-life benefits of embracing a more life-affirming model of disability both as individual parents and as the community of the ecclesia. It closes with some discussion over beginning and end of life issues in relation to disability and the messages these send to people with disabilities. It is the conviction of Brock and Swinton that with the rate of technological advance, science needs the church as a moral anchor.

Chapter 8 seeks to open up some pastoral issues for families with children with disabilities. A particular focus is on fathers and their needs at a time of trauma when most support is for the mother. Material is taken from a number of books and articles relating to the family and disability, and from the Fatherhood Institute which exists as a policy advisor and offers considerable advice on the support of dads. The question of increased risk of divorce is discussed, and while there is some truth to this claim it is seen to have been greatly exaggerated, and a source of additional threat to parents newly adjusting to the reality of a disabled child. The need for communities of interdependence is underlined here along with other special support networks for mothers and fathers individually and for couples together to strengthen the marriage.

References

Aspis, S. (1991), 'Reclaiming the Social Model of Disability', London: BSA Conference paper: GLAD.

Barnes, C. (1991), *Disabled People in Britain and Discrimination: A case for anti-discrimination legislation*, London: Hurst.

Clack, B. (1999), *Misogyny and the Western Philosophical Tradition*, New York: Routledge.

Driedger, D. (1989), *The Last Civil Rights Movement: Disabled People's International*, London: Hurst.

Finkelstein, V. (1980), *Attitudes and Disability: Issues for discussion*, New York, World Rehabilitation Fund.

Finkelstein, V. (1981), 'To deny or not to deny disability', in Brechin, A., Liddiard, P. and Swain, J., *Handicap in a Social World*, London: Hodder and Stoughton.

French, S. (1993), 'Can you see the Rainbow? The roots of denial', in Swain, J., Finkelstein, V., French, S. and Oliver, M. (eds), *Disabling barriers – Enabling Environments*, London: Sage, pp. 69–77.

French, S. (1993), 'Disability, impairment or something in between?' in Swain, J., Finkelstein, V., French, S. and Oliver, M., *Disabling Barriers – Enabling Environments*, London: Sage, pp. 17–25.

Jones, S. (2000), *Feminist Theory and Christian Theology*, Minneapolis: Fortress Press.

Leach, B. (1991), 'Disabled people and the implementation of local authorities' Equal Opportunities Policies', in *Disability & Society* 6(3), pp. 219–31.

Oliver, M. (1993), 'Re-defining disability: A challenge to research', in Swain, J., Finkelstein, V., French, S. and Oliver, M., *Disabling Barriers – Enabling Environments*, London: Sage, pp. 61–7.

Storkey, E. (1985), *What's Right with Feminism*, London: SPCK.

Walmsley, J. (1993), 'Talking to top people: Some issues relating to the citizenship of people with learning disabilities', in Swain, J., Finkelstein, V., French, S. and Oliver, M., *Disabling Barriers – Enabling Environments*, London: Sage, pp. 257–65.

Young, F. (1990), *Face to Face: A narrative essay in the theology of suffering*, Edinburgh: T & T Clark.

Disability in Historical Perspective

Think about the following questions *before* reading this chapter. After reading Chapter 2 you will return to some modification of them.

- What was your first encounter with disability?
- How did it make you feel or what were your thoughts at the time?
- Have further encounters changed the way you understand disability?

There is wisdom in the notion that to see more clearly where we are headed we need to take a long hard look at the journey thus far. In this chapter we will look at early civilizations, the Classical world of the Greeks and Romans, and then explore our British culture from Medieval times up to and including the Victorian era, post world wars and into the present. This may not be easy reading for those with twenty-first-century sensibilities of disability that has been radically redefined by the philosophical shifts of post-modernity. This historical overview will enable us to grasp how one model of disability gained a hegemonic dominance until very recent times. Further, Judaeo-Christian thinking will be a point for particular attention, including the historical Jesus, given the criticisms that have frequently been levelled at Judaeo-Christian faith by the largely secular Disability Movement (see definition on page 25), and indeed sometimes from within the Judaeo-Christian community itself.

It is crucial that the reader understands that while impairment has always been a reality of human life, disability as a category has not, and the moral understanding of the subject has been a matter of dispute for some time and tends to differ across eras and cultures. This chapter therefore requires the reader to be aware of unexamined, subconscious assumptions they may have regarding disability, and to be willing to challenge them. Since religion is part of our worldview, it should not be surprising that some negative values are inscribed in religious texts and traditions, and that these need to be re-examined under the microscope.

Ancient Civilizations

Edwards (1995, p. 166) makes the important point that although western people are accustomed to regarding disabled people as a distinct group, this was not so in the Ancient world. Information about disabled people in the Ancient Near East is difficult to uncover precisely because they were integrated into society. A community model of disability is likely to be the reason, as they were not isolated as a separate group but fully integrated into the rural life.

Starting our brief exploration with ancient civilizations, we note cave paintings dating back as far as 30,000 years which depict the strongest and fittest warriors; and yet juxtaposed with these symbols of strength are people transfigured as part human and part beast; some with additional heads, wings or malformed feet (Wallman 2001, p. 47). Furthermore, ancient Babylonian tablets depict humans who appear to have congenital defects engaged in ritual practice. This is totally counter-intuitive since in Babylonian society the birth of a defective child was generally regarded as an evil omen for the family. Hence, examination of the foetal remains and defects of a born child was a common form of divination seeking to establish the deeper relevance of the birth for the family and wider society. Views typical of the pre-scientific era include the notion that the reason for deformity was either a shock received by the mother during pregnancy or, turning to the father, the quantity of semen (too little or too much) used in conception.

The Sumerian myth of Enki and Ninmah is an attempt to

incorporate people with disabilities into the social structure and thus presupposes a community model of disability (Avalos 2007, p. 19). A diviner had to be perfect in body so even squinting eyes and chipped teeth could prove to be barriers to the priesthood, such was the demand for perfection (p. 26).

The Classical World

The Classical world is of particular interest since the foundations of western civilization and culture were laid by the Ancient Greeks and account for a particular bias in western society, as outlined by the blind cleric Jane Wallman:

> The value system of the democracy we have inherited was founded on concepts of order and degree; balance, symmetry, images of perfection and beauty. Disablement, by its nature, is the antithesis of much that was held precious in Greek and Roman culture, for it encapsulates dependency, uncertainty and weakness. (2001, p. 51)

The achievement of the Greeks in terms of philosophy, arts and architecture has had a profound effect on western culture. The lack of access for people with mobility impairments has its origins in the influence of Greek architecture on building design in Europe and America. Although the Greeks are credited with asserting citizenship rights and the dignity of the individual, these were never intended to be universally extended either to women or indeed to any non-Athenians.

In this society physical and intellectual fitness was highly prized, so there was no room for those with imperfect bodies. In his study of deformity and disability in the Graeco-Roman world Garland (1995) comments that in the arts the Greeks, and Romans to a lesser degree, gave the impression to an outsider that physiological perfection was consistent with their lived reality. Yet 10 per cent of the population was affected by disability from an early age, a fact of which the culture seemed to be in denial.

In addition, the concept of stigma comes from the Greek custom of marking or burning a person to indicate they were a slave. The Greek obsession with bodily perfection led to excessive measures such as infanticide for children born with impairments, or indirect infanticide through exposure to the elements, as required by law in Sparta.

The Greek gods and goddesses were the models that all were encouraged to emulate, and notably only one had an impairment, a limp: Hephaestes (the son of Hera and Zeus). Zeus effectively practises infanticide by banishing him from heaven. The rest of his fate has implications for some of society's unfounded assumptions about sexual virility and disability. He was made to marry Aphrodite who was subsequently repeatedly unfaithful to him.

Disability and deformity as subjects for amusement were advanced by Cicero in his treatise 'On Oratory 2.239', in which he states that these traits provide good material for making jokes (Avalos et al. 1995, p. 39).

Medieval Era

In tracing the origins of attitudes to disabled people, Finkelstein (1980, 1981) gives a compelling explanation of how disabled people came to be segregated from everyday life. He claims that before the Industrial Revolution, disabled people were easily accommodated in the pastoral life of a feudal society. This meant they were integrated within their communities having a number of legitimate social and economic roles that included 'the village idiot' or 'beggar', roles that subsequently disappeared. They were part of an undifferentiated mass of poor, but were not excluded from their non-disabled peers and were known as persons. While a number of writers agree with Finkelstein, that life in pre-industrial societies was more accommodating for disabled people, Borsay takes issue with him. Quoting a Quaker cloth merchant in 1714 promoting the work ethic, he concludes: 'Given such espousal of the work ethic, the pre-industrial labour market may not have been very hospitable to impaired participants' (2002, p. 104).

The work ethic is one thing, but the introduction of industrial time is quite another. John Swinton enlightens us on this matter in *Becoming Friends of Time*. He asserts that as the workplace became overpowered by the speed of the free market economy the efficient use of time was assumed to be normative. '*As time became money so the disabled became a burden and a handicap*' (italics mine) (2016, p. 43).

Coupled with this, the introduction of mechanization led to a more regimented way of working. Equipment was designed for use by a 'standard' operator so that people with impairments found themselves increasingly excluded from the workforce and the social milieu. Also the pace of work was less amenable for disabled people. Essentially any flexibility that may have existed previously was squeezed out. Although it is clear that the Industrial Revolution was detrimental to disabled people, Barnes claims that there is evidence of a consistent bias against people with impairments in western society before the advent of capitalism.

So capitalism alone does not seem to offer a full explanation of the bias against disabled people. The matter is worsened by the simple fact that voices of disabled people in history are largely silent. However, let us turn to anthropology and then to feminist theory to discover deeper-rooted reasons for this primeval intolerance.

Anthropologist, Mary Douglas underlines that our perception and attitude to impairment and disability is heavily influenced by a deep-seated psychological fear of the unknown, the 'abnormal' and the anomalous. In concord with this psychological view, and going further, feminist theorists speak of 'othering', where society is hostile to those they see as simply different from themselves. The concept has its origin in the idea of 'the male as norm' in society so that women are seen as a threat because they are 'other than men' despite being a known quantity as mothers, sisters, wives, etc. This suspicion of the 'other' it is argued, is at the root of racism and a raft of other 'isms' common in today's world.

The Medieval Synthesis

Focusing more now on theology than history, we will consider the Medieval synthesis. Two prominent theologians sought to create a synthesis between Christianity and the Classical worldview: Aquinas merging Christian thought with the work of Aristotle, and Augustine melding Christianity with Plato. It could be argued that much of the liberatory thrust of Christianity was lost in this synthesis. Christianity strayed from what had been handed down by the apostles and taught by the Church Fathers and Mothers. As we have seen Graeco-Roman culture held a very negative view of those disabled from birth. Aristotle introduced the spurious idea of inferior and superior human beings. Critics of Christianity tend to have a Medieval model in mind when they lay all the ills of the modern world at its door. However, we must bear in mind that western culture, which critics often conflate with Christianity, is built on the Classical model and primitive Christianity shared the Oriental influences of Jewish culture, and thus is more eastern than western.

My intention here is to recover the purity of that original Judaeo-Christian vision rather than to jettison it and embrace a secular model that will not be able to deliver as it cannot address the core issue of the human heart and its need of radical reform.

Judaeo-Christian Perspectives

The Judaeo-Christian worldview rests on belief in an infinite and personal God who has spoken directly through the Old Testament prophets and revealed himself fully through the person and teachings of Jesus Christ. The knowledge of God held by Jews and Christians rests on revelation rather than on speculation. They have always lived by values that are absolute, which brought the early Christians into bloody conflict with Rome as they refused to worship Caesar as God, insisting that Jesus Christ alone is to be worshipped.

Some biblical texts are open to very negative interpretations and many writers, including Pentecostal theologian Amos Yong (2007, p. 42), caution against a mere surface reading as the plain interpretation of some texts has been oppressive to people with disabilities over centuries. Yong believes that a 'redemptive theology of disability for our time' must go beyond this.

Jewish psychologist Ellen Wertlieb shows how a deeper understanding can sometimes throw up some very unexpected interpretations.

Wertlieb takes seriously the claim, assumption even, that Judaeo-Christian thinking has given rise to a negative construction of disability. It is popular to make such claims, and American disability activist, Nancy Eiseland, states that such fashionable claims fail to take into account the growing body of liberation theology that Christians draw on to reconceptualize disability and insist on God's preferential option for the poor. Wertlieb insists that these claims with regard to disability have never been systematically researched and she sets out to conduct an in-depth analysis of Talmudic sources and finds the evidence to be very far from conclusive of those claims.

Wertlieb starts the debate with an astounding and incontestable fact:

> This stress on being 'unblemished' is an enigma in light of the fact that many of our Jewish heroes were, in fact, disabled. Issac, for example, was blind during most of his adult life; Leah was visually impaired (Henkin 1983) and Moses had a speech impediment (Gruber 1986). (1988, p. 193)

This list does not include Jacob who startlingly *becomes* disabled as a direct result of his encounter with God.

A further difficulty arises regarding our assumption that anything to do with priesthood is connected with privilege and therefore desirable. Wertlieb shows us the Hebrew understanding of the priestly office.

> According to the Talmud 'they who sacrifice are regarded the same as those which are sacrificed' (Zevahim 16b). Since this

statement suggests that the priests are regarded as objects, it can be argued that they are not, in fact, being treated on a higher level than individuals who have disabilities. (1988, p. 193)

Therefore, the prohibition in Leviticus 21.17 'None of your descendants who has a defect may come near to offer the food of his God' must be read through this understanding.

However, Wertlieb looks at the Talmud and how the rabbis were inclined to interpret the Torah and rule on that basis, and the practices uncovered offer some refreshing surprises. Wertlieb unpacks the practice and regulations regarding blind people serving as judges (1988, p. 206). She surmizes that the practice of Rabbi Shesheth to accept such evidence was most likely motivated by his own experience of blindness and his consequent struggle for equality. The presence of blind Talmudic rabbis at these debates is also seen as having a positive impact.

If it is concluded that the Hebrew texts are not discriminatory of disabled persons per se, what then could be the reason for this emphasis on physical perfection? Wertlieb, characteristically, has two important things to say on this, based partly on an in-depth analysis of the Hebrew language, and also on her psychological expertise. Numbers 25.12 is controversial for translators as it can read 'covenant of peace' but equally can be translated 'covenant of perfection'. Wertlieb points out that it is likely that the two terms have been conflated, for the root for Shalom (peace) and schelmut (wholeness) is the same namely, SH-L-M; there being no vowel sounds in written Hebrew. She argues therefore that the unblemished priest symbolizes the power that enables us to overcome our differences and impairments – a power that we all have, and have need of. Essentially it is about the freedom we have to establish new personal identities (Omer-Man, quoted in Wertlieb 1988). From her psychological background she links this to Maslow's hierarchy of needs:

the unblemished priest can be viewed as representing an inward striving that we have to be 'whole' human beings.

This physical symbol of 'wholeness' may signify what Maslow (1968) describes as the human need to become self-actualized and develop one's potential so as to live a rewarding and fulfilling life. (1988, p. 194)

We will now consider the figure of the historical Jesus and the Gospel accounts which have occasionally been problematic for some in the disability community.

The Historical Jesus and Disability

This first section considers the historical figure of Jesus Christ and his praxis regarding inclusion. This will be explored in the context of first-century Judaism and the Jewish tradition.

The Jewish world was a theological patchwork, although there were some consistent themes, notably, the nature of holiness. The prophetic writings of the Old Testament especially of Isaiah (sometimes known as the fifth Gospel) depict a view of YHWH as inclusive and universalistic, reaching out with salvation to the ends of the earth (Isa. 49.6). Nevertheless, some other parts of the Old Testament, for example, the books of Ezra and Nehemiah focus on the exclusivity of God's covenant with Israel. At the time of Jesus, Judaism was struggling with the issue of how to reconcile exclusivism and inclusivism.

Furthermore, the world into which Jesus was born was dominated by four main groups: Pharisees, Priests/Sadducees, Zealots and Essenes. The Zealots mounted an armed resistance to Rome and Jesus made clear, when Peter cut off the ear of the soldier during his arrest, that violence had no place in his kingdom (John 18.10–11). The Essenes sought to withdraw from society waiting an apocalyptic end that would deal with their enemies. The Pharisees and Priests/Sadducees shunned contact with the masses for reasons of ritual purity, believing the 'ends of the earth' to be a place of chaos, in sharp contrast to the temple. The Pharisees and Sadducees/Priests all sought ritual purity, the former through obedience to the Torah in the synagogues and the latter through cultic obedience in the temple.

Although Jesus confirmed the permanence of the whole Torah (Matt. 5.17–19) he was more interested in adhering to the deeper meanings than a mere conformity to a surface understanding of the requirements of the law (see Jesus remarks on adultery, Matt. 5.27–28).

Wright describes the society of the Pharisees as 'angrily insisting on its own purity towards outsiders' (1996, p. 36). Theirs was a strict adherence to surface matters which led to a form of nationalistic xenophobia. Interestingly, the word 'sinner' was itself a term used primarily by the Pharisees and refers to those who 'did not accept in practice the Pharisaic programme of holiness for Israel and could not be trusted with tithing and cleanliness' (Borg 1995, p. 84). Jesus enraged the Pharisees because he was proclaiming this extravagant welcome to himself as pivotal to the coming Kingdom, in marked contrast to the elitist expectations of the Pharisees. Both the Torah which was the law of the priests, and the Dead Sea Scrolls of the Qumran Community revealed the practice of excluding people with bodily imperfections (Lev. 21.18) (1QM 7.4–6). Qumran aimed to create a restored community by excluding people with disabilities (Wright 1996, p. 46).

The inclusivity found in Isaiah appears to have been forgotten by these main groups but significantly, not by Jesus. The inclusivism of Jesus was very much concerned with returning people to the circle of fellowship within the community. When he healed the man with leprosy (Mark 1.44) Jesus sent him back to the temple to offer a sacrifice thus drawing him back into the practices that the Torah indicated and from which he had been excluded while leprous. This appears to be the main thrust of many of the healings that Jesus performed. He demonstrated philozenia (love of outsiders) showing a radical openness to others: speaking with women as seen with the Samaritan woman (John 4); reaching out to the Syro-Phoenician woman (Mark 7.26); engaging with Gentiles as for example, the Gadarene 'demoniac' (Mark 5.1–20), enjoying table fellowship with sinners and befriending tax collectors (Mark 2.13–17). Jesus differed in his values from all the main Jewish groups: he upheld non-violent resistance, engagement

with the world, rather than withdrawal, he practised acceptance of outsiders and freedom from oppression to insiders
(Wright 1996, p. 39), and a concern for absolute personal
integrity rather than a superficial appearance of holiness.
Since Jesus' own holiness was not based on surface matters he
happily mixed with outcasts thus making himself ceremonially
unclean. His holiness was so intrinsic that he did not fear con-
tamination, rather when Jesus touched someone unclean (for
example, lepers) they received his wholeness.

Luke's Gospel with its beatitudes and woes (Luke 6.20–26)
reveals a 'preferential option for the poor', but Jesus seems
to involve himself with some notably rich people, thus ruling
out the most obvious interpretation of 'the poor'. After a full
exploration of the possible meanings, Green states 'in the Third
Gospel, "good news to the poor" is pre-eminently a gracious
word of inclusion to the dispossessed, the excluded'. Economic
matters are seen to be less significant than issues of status and
honour (Green 1994, p. 69).

From this it can be seen that most of the Jewish groups were
exclusive while Jesus practised a radical inclusivity. Jesus is
reported to have healed a good number of people. Borg (1995,
p. 55) notes 'the stories of his healings shatter the purity boundaries of his social world'.

We can now turn to the important related issue of Jesus
healings and the issues they bring out in relation to the contemporary disability agenda: namely, why was it necessary
for people to be healed rather than simply being accepted as
they were? This lament is based on the understanding of many
disabled people that the impairment as such can be handled
but the discrimination and social exclusion cannot. Some wish
that Jesus had 'healed' the structural sins and prejudices of the
society instead of concentrating on a few individuals.

Post-colonial disability theologian Sharon Betcher objects:
'there's something about that healing touch of Jesus and its
ability to disappear us that persons with disabilities have come
to suspect, especially in terms of using us for its own narrative
conclusions' (2007, p. 79). This critical reading of Jesus' healing miracles is not supported by the theological understanding

of the significance of miracles found in the Gospels. In Mark 2.9 we find the story of Jesus healing a paralysed man. He says: 'Your sins are forgiven' and then 'Take your mat and walk'. At first blush this story appears to forge the popular link between sin and disability which is understandably objectionable. However, Tim Keller suggests that Jesus is highlighting that we all need to be freed from the power of sin even if we are otherwise fine (2011, p. 28). Seeing sin as the real problem is a universalizing response which does not put people with impairments in a different league to the rest of humanity. For further exploration of this see Chapter 5 of this book.

Furthermore, in the healing narrative of the blind man in John 9 Jesus *expressly refutes* the folkloric link between sin and disability when his disciples ask him to comment on whose sin has brought about the man's infirmity. However, the rest of his answer 'so that the works of God might be displayed in him' raises new objections: the usual ableist interpretation of this is that Jesus is using the man's blindness as an opportunity to display his power. Nevertheless, some believers with impairments, notably Grant regard Jesus' statement 'that the son of God might be glorified' as indicating not so much the healing of the man but his transformation into a disciple (1998, p. 84). 'We can see him as an ordinary human being moved to witness to Jesus Christ in the service of God' (p. 86).

In Mark 7.25–30 Jesus reaches out to the Syro-Phoenician woman, healing her daughter. The fact that he appears to call her 'a dog' (a common insult used by the Pharisees towards the Gentiles) does not imply disrespect, for the word Jesus uses is a diminutive form meaning 'puppy'. Jesus is speaking in parables and the woman gets the point that in families, the pets eat too, but not before the children have eaten (Keller 2011, p. 87). Jesus is demonstrating the inclusive view of Isaiah for salvation to be first to the Jews and then to the Gentiles: a point made in the version found in Matthew 15.24. Jesus may want to observe an order here but no one is to be denied their requests. As a woman and a Gentile she is a double outsider, yet Jesus shows her kindness and compassion. Some have commented on the healing of the profoundly deaf man in Mark 7.31–37 as making most sense if Jesus is using a form of sign language: putting his fingers in his ears and touching his tongue. Also taking him aside from the crowd shows sensitivity to the likelihood that the man is used to being made into a spectacle and Jesus is refusing to treat him in this way.

Many current objections to the healing narratives involve an anachronistic reading, reading back into the texts of the first century a modern concern with the cult of normalcy which is intrinsically linked to capitalist societies and thus involves an overlay from the nineteenth to twenty-first centuries on to the texts. It is important to note that for the early Christians, miracles were indications of the advent of the messianic age and a sign of the restoration of right relation of an individual with a community, with God and not least with themselves thus making inclusion possible. Jesus is interested in restoring people to the circle of fellowship where they can flourish.

Historically, Jesus shows a remarkable concern for inclusion that is usually reflected in the ideals, though by no means always the practices, of the Christian church. The Kingdom of God is an inclusive community: God's love and grace breaks all boundaries: national, cultural, gender, disability and so on, as Paul strikingly writes, 'There is neither Jew nor Gentile, neither slave nor free, nor is there male and female, for you are all one in Christ Jesus' (Gal. 3.28).

We see from the discussion so far, that Judaeo-Christian thinking is not disablist per se. Yet as we have seen in the Medieval era a different situation exists on account of an unholy alliance between Classical thought and a Judaeo-Christian worldview.

Up to and Including the Victorian Era

With regard to English history, the exclusion of disabled people from familiar settings coincided with the introduction of segregated institutions and asylums. The primary Victorian rationale for dealing with disability was containment A further negative consequence of industrialization was the separation between work and home which caused the boundaries of family obligations towards disabled people to be redrawn. Sadly, in this situation the emergence of asylums and workhouses met a legitimate need among poor families who now more than ever before were in danger of being overwhelmed by the burden of care. Oliver (1990) also notes that a further consequence of this social separation was that 'disability became a thing of shame'.

A statute in 1388 mandated local officials to differentiate between the deserving and the undeserving poor. Nevertheless, although people with impairments were among the deserving poor they were not really separated from the rest of the community of poor.

In the sixteenth century the church became poorer and weaker on account of a series of unsuccessful political confrontations with the monarchy. An increasing demand for charity resulted from an increase in the vagrant population in England due to poor harvests, the plague and immigration from Ireland and Wales. The Tudor monarchs were obliged to make some economic provision for those dependent on charity and the 1601 Poor Law Act was the first step in recognizing a need for the public authorities to intervene in the lives of disabled people.

The eighteenth and nineteenth centuries were marked by an intensified oppression of disabled people and can be attributed to the prevailing ideologies of the era which emphasized the rights of individuals over the group or state, in relation to culture, politics and property rights. The publication of Darwin's *Origin of Species* in 1859 was sometimes used to provide a 'scientific' authentication. On Darwinism, Barnes contends that 'it had an understandable appeal to a society dominated by a relatively small elite of property-owning, self-interested, "rational" individuals who welcomed any opportunity to justify their newly acquired wealth, status and power' (1991, p. 19).

This 'scientific' view was swiftly applied to human societies and 'social Darwinism' provided the justification not to assist the disadvantaged as their sufferings were seen as the inevitable outcome of progress.

The 1868 Poor Law Amendment Act introduced improvements for education by allowing any deaf and dumb child, or
blind child, to be sent to any school suited to their needs. In
1885 The Royal Commission on the Blind, Deaf and Dumb
was set up and four years later it reported that this provision
had not been implemented due to education being regarded as
a charitable concession rather than a duty: thus the provision
was not compulsory. As a consequence of this report, in the
early 1890s, Education of Blind and Deaf-Mute Children Acts
were passed and schooling was later extended to include those
with less visible impairments such as epilepsy.

The Royal Commission decreed that if poor families were
unable to provide for the cost of education for their disabled
children then the responsibility should fall to the school board
of the parish to pay out of the school fund for the necessary elementary schooling. This position indicated a shift in Victorian
policy from containment as the primary response to disability,
to philanthropy and compensation. Some of the philanthropic
institutions had names such as: 'Guild of the Brave Poor
Things', 'The Crutch and Kindness League' and 'The League
of Hearts and Hands'. Those who were not drawn into such
establishments continued to become victims of the Poor Law,
being forced into the workhouse, or imprisoned under the
vagrancy laws for those who were homeless.

One further move in the Victorian era that Drake (1999)
claims was related to disability was legislation introduced to
deal with the disabling consequences of accidents with machinery. In 1897 and 1900 there were Workmen's Compensation
Acts which held employers legally responsible to compensate
their employees for industrial accidents. Other measures
sought to regulate the use of dangerous machinery such as the
Chaff-cutting Machines Act of 1897. Under Queen Victoria's
rule aid was offered to disabled people in very limited ways
and injury at work was one of the prime contexts for help.
However, one could argue that these acts were aimed at
protecting the interests of able-bodied people who may incur
disability rather than offering support to disabled people per
se. However, one area of support for disabled people, as we

have seen, was the provision of elementary schooling, but even this was a mixed blessing as it was through education policies that disabled children first came to be segregated from their non-disabled peers. In 1890 the Education of Blind and Deaf-Mute Children Act (Scotland) made provision for separate schools to be built. The Education Act of 1921 then obliged parents to make use of these specialized schools.

Furthermore, people with cognitive impairments fared particularly badly as between 1837–1901 there were in excess of 20 measures addressing 'insanity' and they were included under that umbrella. The Lunacy Legislation of 1845 empowered doctors to dictate where people with mental health needs could live and to move them around against their will. Barnes (1991) traces the dominance of the medical profession in all aspects of disability back to this point. In 1886 the term 'idiot' was formally introduced for such people in the establishing of the Idiots Act. In 1896 the National Association for the Care and Control of the Feeble-minded was set up as a pressure group for the lifetime segregation of people with mental impairments. The situation was worsened by the invention of Intelligence Quotient tests by the French psychologists Binet and Simon and their widespread use, as leading psychologists, notably Cyril Burt, made strong assertions to the effect that IQ was innate and therefore fixed and that 'the majority of defectives were ineducable' (Barnes 1991, p. 19). Children with mental impairments were excluded from schooling under the 1944 Education Act and it was not until 1970 that an Act was introduced to give the right to an education to children with special educational needs.

The Modern Era

After two world wars, a shift began to occur concerning views on disability. However, this was largely due to large numbers of soldiers returning as amputees or with other impairments. The collective national guilt led to measures of compensation for injured soldiers yet sadly this forced disabled citizens to the back of the queue as far as jobs, housing and health care were concerned.

Divisive attitudes among the population took hold. Drake states that the war wounded were regarded as 'unnaturally abnormal' whereas disabled civilians were seen as 'naturally abnormal'.

In the inter-war years a new area of segregation opened up with the advent of orthopaedic hospitals. Childhood impairments lessened on account of the lower incidence of rickets and tuberculosis and rehabilitation became the new focus. There are glowing reports (Watson 1930) about what could be achieved through surgery yet these are written by outsiders to the experience and are in sharp contrast to some other accounts by the now adult children who endured these 'medical advances' and who write of 'torture' and 'unending torment' (Borsay 2002, p. 113).

The twentieth century ushered in an era of increased political suffrage until 1929 when all British citizens over the age of 21 were entitled to vote with the caveat that they must be 'of sound mind'. Walmsley (2013) comments that at this time people with learning disabilities were denied both political and civil rights. It is important to note that on the equal opportunities agenda people with intellectual impairments were very low down, that is, even if they featured at all.

In 1948 welfare-based services were introduced through the advent of the National Assistance Act and developed fast over the next two decades. In some respects disability first became a social category at this time as people were categorized according to their needs for provision. As we have seen, up to this point disabled people were just part of the general mass of humanity and not distinguished from others in the community. The 'Community Care' policy (1990) led to a growth in social services. This was not a good move for disabled people as the private sector was placed in charge so disabled people still had no control over their own lives.

The Seebohn report (1968) is generally seen as a watershed in the development of community-based provision for disabled people. Subsequent Acts were based on these recommendations and local authorities were empowered to offer domestic help, hot dinners and transport for holidays. Making public places accessible became important. During this period there was a robust fight for a disability income to give disabled people the same range of options as their non-disabled peers.

At the end of the 1970s the outgoing Labour government had set up a committee on restrictions against disabled people. Published in 1982, according to Drake, the report found evidence of significant discrimination, but the incoming Conservative government was dismissive of the findings.

Drake also claims that in the 1980s social services were under a Thatcherite cloud and pressure was applied to reduce rather than enhance provision.

Recent Attitudes

Thus, in the nineteenth century, there was some very heavy-handed legislation that denied freedom of choice regarding schooling for disabled children or accommodation for adults with mental health needs. This issue of personal freedom and dignity has been high on the agenda in recent times. Since the 1970s there has been a significant move away from the representation of disabled people by charitable organizations who spoke for disabled people towards self-determination and self-advocacy. The International Disabled People's Movement politicized disability (Davis 1993; Driedger 1989; Oliver 1990) and since that time a number of academics, some of whom are themselves disabled, have reconceptualized disability as a complex form of social oppression. Analysis has moved from a focus on individuals and their impairments to a disabling society that erects physical barriers in addition to oppressive social attitudes and values. The institutional oppression of disablism is not dissimilar to racism, sexism or heterosexism, although, of course, it may also intersect with any or all of these. However, this academic group may have further marginalized people with intellectual impairments, creating something of a hierarchy of disability with intellectual competence at the top. For this reason, I choose to foreground this latter group. Interestingly though, some prominent intellectual Christian thinkers who write on disability, including Stanley Hauerwas, Frances Young, John Swinton, Amos Yong, Jean Vanier, Henri Nouwen and Hans Reinders have championed the cause of people with intellectual impairments especially arguing for their *centrality* in the Christian church.

It has been argued that The International Disabled People's Movement is the last human rights campaign, the aims of which have been summed up in an adaptation of a well-known phrase 'to boldly go where everyone else has gone before' (Abberley 1996, p. 159), and this goal is, perhaps, epitomized in the movement's demand for independent living. The movement in this country consists of issue-specific lobby groups, direct action coalitions and a network of grassroots organizations, all run by disabled people themselves under the leadership of the British Council of Disabled People (BCODP). The British Council of Disabled People is the British arm of The International Disabled People's Movement. As Britain's national umbrella organization for groups controlled by disabled people, between them the 120 member groups now have a total membership of around 300,000.

In line with rejecting a passive and tragic view of disability, some developments have included acts of civil disobedience carried out by people with impairments, and the advent of the Disability Arts Movement which has been instrumental in creating a more positive image of people with impairments. The Disability Arts Movement is one of the most progressive developments for disabled people to date, as according to Hevey (2013) it is the first sign of a post-tragedy disability culture and is addressing the cultural vacuum created by this paradigm shift.

In conclusion, it must be stated that disability in the present day is no longer seen as a matter of charity but of human rights. This has been an important shift and has led to some key thinkers building further upon it. For example, McCloughry (2002) argues for rights not charity but Swinton (2016) building on that says that it is a matter not of politics but of love. It might appear that we have come full circle but 'charity' has come to mean something very different from the root word 'caritas' which denotes a respectful dignified love. Tataryn explains:

> Charity ... creates a power differential and belittles the receivers of alms. In contrast caritas, responds with compassion to the needs of equals, caring less for self than for the relief of another. We witness caritas in the early church and in the development of monasticism ... Our community based in caritas is the dwelling place of the living Christ: this sacred space is sanctuary. (2013, pp. 118–19)

So we might say that the shift that Swinton is arguing for is more for caritas than either charity or the political language of rights which does nothing to change the human heart with its proclivities to exclusion.

We are now ready to explore the various models of disability as a grasp of the theory is essential if we are to foster good practice.

Points for Discussion and/or Reflection

1 What surprised you most in the history of disability?
2 Which of these views have influenced you most?

Linguistic choices

A slogan of the Disability Movement has been *'nothing about us without us'* and this is a constraining factor in selecting which linguistic terms to use. It would be naive, as some are (Chryssavagis 2002, and others), to assume that the DM speaks with one voice on terminology for disabled people. Hunt (1966); Harrison (1995) and others object to phrases like 'the blind', 'the deaf', etc., as they imply a group outside the rest of society. Generally 'people/persons with disabilities' is preferred as it foregrounds that we are talking about a person and the disability is secondary. However, Oliver (1990) objects to anything that suggests disability is an add on rather than an integral part of a person, thus preferring 'disabled person'. Others would object to this term as society is thought to be the only disabling factor in creating disabled persons. In this case 'impaired' is preferred over 'disabled'.

In this book terms will be used interchangeably so as to minimize offence. The need to respect the *feelings* of people with disabilities is uppermost in this endeavour and may be at odds with a deeper understanding of linguistics.

The term 'handicapped' seems to be universally disapproved of now as it depicts a beggar 'going cap in hand'. Etymologically, 'handicap' was originally a game, a kind of lottery, in which the winner paid a forfeit, the umpire held the money in his hand in a cap. Later the term came to be used in relation to competition in which the unequal competitors were weighted so as to make the match more equal. Thus the word has connotations of competition and efforts to create equality (Ingstad and Reynolds Whyte 1995, p. 7). Some people have played with the term creating such words as 'handicapable' or 'handicopeable'. However, Govig objects to this 'whitewashing of reality' (1989, p. 9).

In recent years the phrase 'learning difficulty' has been replaced by 'learning disability' and this allows for differentiation between such things as dyslexia and dyspraxia which can be called 'learning difficulties', while 'learning disability' is the politically correct replacement for 'mental handicap'. However, although 'learning disability' is widely used in the UK and is the accepted term in government documents it should be noted that self-advocacy groups have expressed a preference for 'people with learning difficulties' (Coles 2001, p. 501). However, a positive reason for using the term 'learning disability' is pointed out by Coles:

> the widespread adoption of the terms 'learning' or 'intellectual' disability in the 1990s made a clear statement that it belongs to disability. Linguistic changes both reflect and encourage a tendency to see learning disability as a fit subject for disability studies. (p. 189)

The terminology then has encouraged the inclusion of people with intellectual impairment in the overall Disability Movement and since the main thrust of this work is inclusion, this path will be taken notwithstanding their stated wishes.

A further area in this linguistic minefield is opened up by those who assert the right to define the more powerful dominant able-bodied in new ways. Oliver speaks of 'the self-styled able bodied' (1990), and elsewhere the phrase 'temporarily able-bodied' is used as an acknowledgement that 85 per cent of the population can expect to be disabled either permanently or temporarily at some time in their lives (Bryant and Reynolds 2001, p. 16).

References

Abberley, P. (1996), 'Work, utopia and impairment', in Barton, L. (ed.), *Disability and Society: Emerging issues and insights*, London: Longman, pp. 25-44.

Avalos, H., Melcher, S. J. and Schipper, J. (2007) (eds), *This Abled Body*, Atlanta: Society of Biblical Literature.

Barnes, C. (1991), *Disabled People in Britain and Discrimination: A case for anti-discrimination legislation*, London: Hurst.

Betcher, S. V. (2007), *Spirit and the Politics of Disablement*, Minneapolis: Fortress Press.

Borg, M. (1995), *Meeting Jesus Again for the First Time*, San Francisco: Harper.

Borsay, A. (2002), 'History, Power and Identity', in Barnes, C., Oliver, M. and Barton, L.

(eds), *Disability Studies Today*, pp. 98-119.

Bryant, A. and Reynolds, G. (2001), *Open to All: A Commitment to a Church Accessible to Everyone*, Guildford: Church of England.

Chryssavagis, J. (2002), *The Body of Christ: A Place of Welcome for People with Disabilities*, Minneapolis: Light and Life.

Coles, J. (2001), 'The Social Model of Disability: What does it mean for practice in services for people with learning disabilities?' in *Disability and Society* 16(4), pp. 501-10.

Davis, K. (1993), 'On the Movement', in Swain, J., Finkelstein, V., French, S. and Oliver, M. (eds), *Disabling Barriers, Enabling Environments*, London: Sage, pp. 285-92.

Drake, R. (1999), *Understanding Disability Policies*, Hants and London: Macmillan.

Driedger, D. (1989), *The Last Civil Rights Movement: Disabled People's International*, London: Hurst.

Edwards, M. L. (1995), 'Physical Disability in the Ancient Greek World', PhD thesis, Minneapolis: University of Minnesota.

Eiesland, N. (1994), *The Disabled God*, Nashville: Abingdon Press.

Finkelstein, V. (1980), *Attitudes and Disability: Issues for discussion*, New York: World Rehabilitation Fund.

Finkelstein, V. (1981), 'To deny or not to deny disability', in Brechin, A., Liddiard, P. and Swain, J., *Handicap in a Social World*, London: Hodder and Stoughton.

Garland, R. (1995), *The Eye of the Beholder: Deformity and Disability in the Graeco-Roman World*, London: Duckworth.

Grant, C. (1998), 'Reinterpreting the healing narratives', in Eiseland, N. and Saliers D. (eds), *Disability and the Service of God*, Nashville: Abingdon Press pp. 72-87.

Green, J. (1994), 'Good news to whom? Jesus and the "Poor" in the Gospel of Luke', in

Green and Turner (eds), *Jesus of Nazareth*, Carlisle: Paternoster Press, pp. 59-74.

Govig, S. (1989), *Strong at the Broken Places*, Louisville: John Knox Press.

Harrison, T. (1995), *Disability: Rights and Wrongs*, Oxford: Lion.

Hevey, D. (2013), 'The Tragedy Principle: Strategies for Change in the Representation of Disabled People', in Swain, J., Finkelstein, V., French, S. and Oliver, M., *Disabling Barriers – Enabling Environments*, London: Sage, pp. 116-121.

Hunt, P. (1996), 'A Critical Condition', in Shakespeare, T., *The Disability Reader*, London: Cassell, pp. 7-19.

Ingstad, B. and Reynolds Whyte, S. (1995), *Disability and Culture*, Berkeley: University of California Press.

Keller, T. (2011), *King's Cross*, London: Hodder & Stoughton.

McCloughry, R. and Morris, W. (2002), *Making a World of Difference*, London: SPCK.

Oliver, M. (1990), *The Politics of Disablement*, London: Macmillan.

Swinton, J. (2016), *Becoming Friends of Time*, London: SCM Press.

Tataryn, M. and Trunchan-Tataryn, M. (2013), *Discovering Trinity in Disability*, New York: Orbis Books.

Wallman, J. (2001), *Disability as Hermeneutic: Towards a theology of community*, unpublished thesis, University of Birmingham.

Walmsley, J. (2013), 'Talking to Top People: Some Issues Relating to the Citizenship of People with Learning Disabilities', in Swain, J., Finkelstein, V., French, S. and Oliver, M., *Disabling Barriers – Enabling Environments*, pp. 257-65, London: Sage.

Watson, F. (1930), *Civilisation and the Cripple*, London: Bale.

Wertlieb, E. (1988), 'Attitudes towards disability as found in the Talmud', *Psychology and Judaism*, 12(4), pp. 192Ð213.

Wright, T. (1996), *The New Testament and the People of God*, London: SPCK.

Yong, A. (2007), *Theology and Down Syndrome*, Texas: Baylor University Press.

Summary

In this chapter we have examined the history of disability, focusing first on recent shifts then going back to early civilizations and highlighting the contrasting perspectives of the classical and Judaeo-Christian worldviews. We have then pursued more of the history, including the historical Jesus and first-century Judaism, the Medieval era – together with the Medieval synthesis – then up to and including the Victorian period, the modern era and finally back to the present day. The scene is now set to introduce the models of disability that emerge from these shifting historical contexts.

Models of Disability and Research Methodologies

This chapter explores the major models of disability today. The medical model will be discussed first leading on to the social model and then four other models which can be charted on the spectrum between medical at one end and social at the other. These models are secular and derive from the field of disability studies, and are concerned with people and how we value them. Later in Chapter 3, where we begin to look at personhood and what it means to be human, we will introduce two more recent models that have a theological foundation, and thus further explore reconceptualising disability for the church. The chapter will end with an exploration of appropriate models for disability research including an introduction to the tenets of critical disability research (which includes questions regarding who can conduct research within the disability community and matters of ethics) and then move on to consideration of a suitable methodology for disability research and a debate about qualitative research among those with profound cognitive disabilities, including those who may not have speech.

Definition of the term Disability Movement
(sometimes also known as Disability Rights Movement)

I am using the term Disability Movement in the rather loose way in which it is used in the literature. A quote from Michelle Mason illustrates the point:

> Like many disabled people I have belonged to the Disability
> Movement since childhood. The day I threw away the holy
> water from Lourdes and said to Jesus, 'I think they are miss-
> ing the point' was the day I joined the movement. I was nine
> years old. I did not know if there were any other members
> then, or if it was just me and Him.

Clearly, she is not referring to a formal organization with paid-up
members but to a point on the social map where solidarity is
found among disabled people with a shared perception of the
moral meaning of disability. However, it does seem that there
is a recognized meaning for the term within the movement. It
denotes a social movement with a focus on civil rights, consciousness raising and, in its second phase, the quest for a
collective identity. Not dissimilar then, to the Women's Movement or the Gay Rights Movement and in the same way merely
to be a woman or to be gay does not imply sympathy with the
overt political objectives of the movement.

According to Mike Oliver, the Disability Movement can be
defined by its three distinctive concepts: the social model of
disability, independent living and civil rights.

The Medical Model

The medical model has historically been the dominant model.
In this model the focus is on the individual and the actual
impairment, and the role of society is to 'cure' that person in an
attempt to 'normalize' them back into the able-bodied world or
remove them from society. Historically this has been achieved
through the use of institutionalization whereby control was
taken of the person's life. The goal is conformity to the standards of the non-disabled world or, where not possible, then
exclusion from that world and to facilitate what Miller and
Gwynne (1972) identified as a transition from 'social death

to physical death'. Since this medical view has been seen to stigmatize and even disenfranchise people with disabilities this model is distinctly out of favour with the Disability Movement. Rieser and Mason (1990) state that historically medical interpretations and values have given rise to a view that physical and/or intellectual impairments are the basic cause of disability. In this model the reactions of disabled people to the society and environment that disables them is seen as pathological rather than a healthy response to a multilayered oppression. This model of disability, which positions the individual as dependent and in need of 'care' from others, gives rise to a theory of personal tragedy focusing on the individual and the impairment and seeing disability as a tragic loss or waste of life (see p. 70 for one positive angle on the medical model).

The Social Model

In advancing a critique of the personal tragedy model of disability, the disabled people's movement has formulated a social model that takes a social constructivist perspective. De Jong (1979) formulated the notion that people with impairments are only disabled in as much as the society around is disabling and presents barriers to a full life. Oliver (1983), a wheelchair user and former professor of sociology, coined the phrase 'a social model of disability' which has become the dominant paradigm and repositions disabled people as citizens with rights. Writers on disability are unanimous in their agreement that the experience of disability is a very real form of oppression. Barton (1996, p. 8) insists 'being disabled involves experiencing discrimination, vulnerability and abusive assaults upon self-identity and esteem'.

Hahn defines disability thus:

> Disability stems from the failure of a structured social environment to adjust to the needs and aspirations of citizens with disabilities *rather than* from the inability of a disabled individual to adapt to the demands of society. (1986, p. 128)

Jane Campbell, who was previously Chair of the British Council of Disabled People, insists that the social model is the Disability Movement's main tool for inclusion for 'it demands an approach that wrecks the foundations of society's main solutions to our so-called "problems", rehabilitation, cure, institutionalization and death' (2002, p. 472). It may be helpful to talk in terms of a strong and a weak form of the social model of disability, for those who support the model with reservations are perhaps buying into a weaker form of the model than some others. The model has much to commend itself from a political viewpoint and is clearly more empowering for the Disability Movement. Deborah Creamer (1998, p. 18) notes 'it is important to remember that there is no one perspective that can be called 'the disabled person's perspective'.

Criticisms of the social model of disability

The social model, while being welcomed for putting political and social concerns to the fore, has been criticized from within on a number of counts. Primarily the issue of impairment is contentious. Critics from mainstream sociology insist that the refusal to allow a link between disability and impairment leads to relativism, and that the reification of structural barriers can serve to create a picture that is as incomplete as a traditional medical perspective. Some feminist disability activists state that the denial of bodily reality is a feminist concern and issues from the masculinist bias of the movement. Sally French, a wheelchair user objects to the fact that she is often told that she does not understand what disability is about and that she has internalized the values of an ableist society because she sees impairment as a lived reality. When assistive technologies are being proposed researchers sometimes meet a brick wall when they ask about impairments. Finkelstein argues that even disability organizations do not campaign against the prospect of eliminating impairment. For this reason the social model has been dubbed by some as 'the anti-social model of disability'.

Tom Shakespeare, while broadly supporting the model, claims it is essentialist. Marian Corker also argues that it does not include deaf people as their disability is mediated by language and not structural barriers. Corker also objects to its essentialist materialism. Worryingly, its tendency to put all the blame on to society renders disabled people powerless victims, leaving little room for agency or resistance.

Since the social model privileges people with physical and sensory impairments it has been argued that it does not include people with learning disabilities, or make sense of their experience. With the exception of Simone Aspis (1999) there has been little contribution to the social model literature by people with learning disabilities.

Further Models of Disability

Since there are now so many models of disability we must be selective. We shall now look at four other models of disability that can be charted on a spectrum between the medical and social ends. They are the alliance model, the overcoming model, the minority culture model and the social-relational model.

The alliance model

This model occupies a middle ground in its attempt to combine the medical and social models. While social modellists tend to see the medical model as incompatible with the social model Jane Brett argues for an 'alliance' model that aims for a marriage of the best of both models: overcoming the tendency of the medical model to render disabled people as passive objects and the social model's inclination to individualism and capitalist values (2002). Theologian Amos Yong argues with others for taking from both models as people with intellectual disabilities do not fit well into the social model:

our religious and theological proposals will certainly draw from the best insights of the social model of disability, but I will also suggest that the latter needs the former to ensure the full inclusion of people with intellectual disabilities in the project of social liberation. (2007, p. 116)

The overcoming model

The overcoming model would be located more at the medical end of the spectrum as it focuses on the impairment but in a way that seeks to overcome it and continue life as if it were not a factor to be reckoned with. This model is not favoured by many in the Disability Movement as it is seen as divisive, encouraging people with disabilities not to identify with others 'worse off'. Its aim is to show that disabled people can cope and conform to the demands of the able-bodied world and as such it can lead to a lot of denial and be highly divisive. Telethon and the Paralympics, where disabled people with strong upper bodies compete in sporting events, have been strenuously opposed by some disability groups (who have dubbed them 'supercrips') because they are based on this model. Primarily it is seen to exist to help the 'temporarily able-bodied' cope with their fear and unease.

The minority culture model

The minority culture model in contrast posits that disabled people, like other minority groups are discriminated against through the imposition of the value system of the dominant culture and that they have their own culture of which they are rightly proud. As such this model must be charted at the social model end of the spectrum.

Nancy Eiseland identifies a shift from a disability rights model to a disability culture model within the movement during the 1980s and 90s. However, she is clear that this is contentious, stating that 'debates about both the viability and existence of a distinct culture have raged within the movement'. The reason she gives for this is that it is seen as unnecessarily separatist and not palatable to those who advocate integration into the dominant able-bodied culture. Also she explains that organizations that have both disabled and able-bodied people among their constituents tend to have an integrationist agenda. The failure of religious organizations to even recognize the issue of a distinct disability culture has caused further division between religious groups and activists. Furthermore, Eiseland notes that debates within religious communities about the viability and/or existence of a distinct disability culture have been curiously absent.

A minority culture model is obviously problematic for those who are moving towards an agenda of inclusion. However, it could be argued that there should be no problem if inclusion is envisaged on a different basis from the dominant culture being uncritically accepted as the norm. Eiseland has one more word that the church needs to heed in this connection.

> The disability movement has at its core contested the moral meaning of disability, declaring people with disabilities to be a minority group with a distinct culture. *Whether or not they agree with this definition, religious leaders ignore the moral implications at their peril.* (My emphasis) (1998, p. 224)

Social relational model

In recent times there has been a move towards a social relational model (Thomas 1999; Reindal 2008). Reindal's rationale for the social relational model of disability is that it better conforms to the morality of inclusion because the main issue of the social model, oppression, is not obliterated. He uses a social relational model in response to criticism of 'special needs education' which is objected to on grounds that it draws too much from a medical model of disability. Feminist writer, Carol Thomas advances this model to avoid the conflation of materialist and relational views of the social model of disability, as she sees the relationship between able-bodied and non-disabled people as similar to the patriarchal relationship between men and women with the former being in the ascendant position of power.

The main models can be seen to undergird the various historical views of disability and are central to the domain of disability studies. In recent times more models have been forthcoming especially from those who seek to add a spiritual dimension to the mainly secular view from disability studies. These will be introduced in Chapter 3 where we begin to engage with theological issues.

Conducting Research in Disability Contexts

In common with churches knowing little about the models of disability or indeed the issues raised by the Disability Movement, research methods is another pertinent topic. Many people (myself once included) know nothing about research methods, yet that does not stop us from conducting research, even within education! During my undergraduate study I conducted a piece of research with sixth form students on career choice, intelligence and personality types: i.e. divergent/convergent thinkers. This was a psychology of education dissertation for my BEd degree. I automatically decided to make a questionnaire with little idea of the protocol. I must have had some notion of researcher bias as I made all my questions open ended, thus creating a nightmare for analysis. I was sent to the maths department to sort it out as in one case I had a question that yielded 45 entirely different responses. From this I want to argue that many people have internalized the concept of quantitative research as being the standard methodology and know nothing of its limitations or strengths or indeed what qualitative research methodology brings to the table.

I was once in a church meeting where hot discussion arose concerning the people who lived in the parish and what they wanted of us. It was suggested that some research be conducted. Someone objected that it was a waste of time to keep pushing questionnaires through people's letter boxes. At this point I was a research student on a PhD course so I sought to offer alternative ways of working that might be more fruitful. I commented that questionnaires were not always the best way to do this sort of research and suggested the use of a focus group discussion perhaps held at an Indian Buffet where people could come and eat (set price) as much as they liked thus feeling rewarded for their time (a common criterion among ethical researchers). The suggestion never reached the light of day as it was simply not really comprehended.

So we will begin here by some discussion of the relative merits of quantitative and qualitative research methodology. Then we will explore a critical disability research method as proposed by Moore, Beazley and Maelzer (1998) and make some comparisons between the values of qualitative research and practical theology in order to lead into a discussion and critique of suitable research methods for people with profound learning disabilities.

Research methodology

Qualitative or quantitative?

Although it is true that these two types of methodology are not arch rivals there is a basic incompatibility between them as they emerge from entirely different worldviews. Concepts of knowledge and even reality itself differ vastly and the methods employed are varied as being suited to their respective objectives. Quantitative research involves an empirical investigation of the research question and uses scientific methods. It aims to gather a large amount of data and this is collected and analysed statistically. While the scientific method holds the illusion of 'objectivity' there can be bias in the way in which the results are interpreted.

Researcher bias seen in interpretation of the data

A staggering real-life example is offered from the research of Danish linguist Otto Jesperson in the 1920s. He conducted a piece of research to explore whether men or women were better at reading comprehension. He set a piece of reading for both groups and timed them and then checked their level of comprehension by asking questions regarding the text. He found, counter to the bias of the expectations of his day, that the women were faster at completing the task and also had higher scores for comprehension. Now to the task of interpretation ... Might a twenty-first-century researcher not just conclude in an uncomplicated fashion that the women were superior at this task? With the mindset of his historical location, he surmised that since the heads of men were so full of important things that the data was slow to be assimilated whereas the heads of women being largely empty it was straightforward for them to process the incoming data. He supported his claim with reference to the time it takes to exit a full room against one that is almost empty. There is an essence of logic to his analysis but with the passing of time the current reader will be quick to discern the considerable bias in his interpretation of the empirical data! (Cameron 1988)

Quantitative research issues from a positivist worldview which regards the social world as having one, external meaning independent of human perception. Thus, questions tend to be fixed and closed so that the interview or survey can be replicated with other samples yielding reliable results.

Qualitative research, on the other hand, seeks to uncover underlying meaning and aims to dig deeper in providing insights into the problem. Rather than being scientific it is a naturalistic and phenomenological project. Social reality is seen as multiple and constructed through consciousness. Qualitative methods allow the researcher to access and explore the respondents' perspectives in depth (Usher and Edwards 1994), and allow space and scope for probing and explaining sometimes unexpected perspectives (Berg 1989, p. 6). Cresswell argues that qualitative research is useful in contexts where a complex and detailed understanding of an issue is required (2007, p. 40). It is also used in offering accounts that reflect the complexity of the respondents' experiences and perceptions and to provide richness of data and thick description (Geertz 1973).

While qualitative research is characterized by subjectivity, it is nevertheless subject to the same rigor as all research. It deals with much smaller amounts of data with a more individual basis. Because it cannot be analysed with the use of computer software, it is much more labour intensive so more costly for organizations opting to use it. Questions are also used in this methodology but in a much more open-ended and flexible way. A semi-structured questionnaire may be used to probe an area and the researcher may let the interviewee take the topic off in new directions that are pertinent to the research subject. There is no expectation of the results being generalizable to wider populations as there is in quantitative exploration. Analysing social phenomena involves an interactive process. Qualitative research also makes use of participant observation, narratives, focus group discussion, life histories and case studies.

In addition, the latter type of research methodology dovetails with many of the values of practical theology. This is principally because practical theology starts from the place of lived experience and 'seeks to explore the complex theological and practical dynamics of particular situations in order to enable the development of a transformative and illuminating understanding of what is going on within situations' (Swinton and Mowat 2016, p. xi). Further, Swinton claims that 'practical theology is critical, analytical, frequently prophetic and revelatory' (p. xi). Where practical theology fits within the qualitative research methodology it is seen especially in the category of action research. For further understanding of this overlap see Harshaw (2016, ch. 2) and Swinton and Mowat (2016).

Critical disability research

An engagement with disabled people as part of any research is particularly problematic and demands that the researcher grapple with additional issues. This is because as Moore et al. point out, research is necessarily conducted 'in the shadow of the politics and power games that are by-products of the professional and vocational structures surrounding disabled people' (1998, p. 89).

This section will consider some specific questions relating to research involving people with learning disabilities and finally a number of ethical considerations. All these issues are addressed within a framework of disability research demonstrating an understanding of the principles that inform an *emancipatory/ participatory* approach.

Emancipatory research, a concept coming out of Freire's participatory pedagogy, was formulated by Mike Oliver but has now been contested by its own author (explained later in this chapter). However, where research is carried out, the Disability Movement would prefer it to adhere to the basic principles of emancipatory research.

Jenny Morris says it

> must be based on: empowerment and reciprocity; changing the social relations of research production; changing the focus of attention away from disabled individuals and onto disablist society. (1992, p. 158)

Added to this, Zarb says,

> making researchers directly accountable to disabled people is a fundamental principle of genuine participatory research, (1992, p. 137)

Origins of the Disability Movement

David Pfeiffer (1995) says, regarding the origins of the Disability Movement: 'It can be argued that eugenics caused the rise of the disability movement in reaction to it.'

There is a historical event that gave rise to the current use of the term 'Disability Movement'. In 1981 Rehabilitation International held a conference in Winnipeg, Canada. RI is made up of primarily non-disabled professionals working in the area of disability. At this conference only 200 of the 3,000 delegates were disabled and they asked for a representation of 50 per cent on the board. This was refused and as a result the disabled delegates stormed out and met to form their own organization which they called The Disabled People's International (DPI). The focus of this organization was disabled people running their own organization, and the slogan 'Nothing about us without us' was formulated and widely used. According to McCloughry and Morris (2002, p. 14) it was from this point that the phrase 'the disability movement' became regular currency as it denoted a shift from powerlessness to disabled people feeling empowered and in control of their own lives.

Zarb also identifies 'empowerment' and 'reciprocity' as central, although as Oliver has noted, empowerment is something people must take for themselves and cannot be given by others (Zarb 1992, p. 128). Furthermore,

> Emancipatory research is about the demystification of the structures and processes which create disability and the establishment of a workable 'dialogue' between the research community and disabled people in order to facilitate the latter's empowerment. (Barnes 1992, p. 17)

However, emancipatory research as a means of doing research is in dispute (along with all other forms of research) for the question arises whether it is possible to conduct research, at all, on disabled subjects without objectifying them and thus causing them further oppression. The point of contention then, is the production of research itself, thus Oliver states that he no longer wishes to be involved in research of any type on disability. 'Partnership Research' is an exception to this. It is a university project where an academic works in tandem with a person with learning disabilities in order to privilege their insider perspective. The subject under review is likely to be about learning disabilities. For example Iain Carson of the University of Manchester told me in an email: 'The focus of my research is knowledge production by people with learning disabilities. I'm operating within a participatory paradigm and my research is being conducted entirely in partnership with a person who has learning disabilities. He has been fully involved in the research design, the production of data collection instruments, the collection of data and the analysis of data.'

Academic researchers in disability issues note a common clash of interests between fulfilling the criteria of academic bodies and serving the interests of disabled people (Moore, Beazley and Maelzer 1998). For this reason Zarb suggests we make use of Michelle Fine's (1990) term of doing 'trangressive research' (Zarb 1992, p. 133). When I was doing my doctoral research I found this rather problematic but ensuring that the church and its attitudes towards people with impairments was the main focus of the study was my way of solving the dilemma. In this case disabled people are only involved where insight about the church and its attitude towards them is needed.

The researcher motivation then was to expose any oppressive practices that may be operating through institutional power and equally, to highlight any areas of good practice that may be found. In this respect the subject under review is 'disablist society' and the extent to which the church conforms or resists those dominant values. In this context it is important to take stock of a point insisted on by Moore et al. that 'research which aspires to be participatory and/or emancipatory has to be characterized by rigorous evaluation of questions of control' (Moore, Beazley and Maelzer 1998, p. 13).

Moore et al. suggest some ground rules for conducting

critical disability research. These will now be examined for although ideologically I am sympathetic to this model, there were some pragmatic difficulties with my research because my subjects had learning disabilities, not all of them able to speak. (I would like to note here that thinking has moved on in this area since I did my research and I will draw on the works of John Swinton, Melanie Nind and Jill Harshaw later in this chapter specifically in respect of doing research with people with profound disabilities.)

Returning to the tenets of conducting critical disability research. They are:

- To engage in critical disability research.
- To give voice to the research subjects and take their views seriously.
- To celebrate subjectivity.
- To ensure that the research leads to improvement for disabled people.
- To own up to a commitment to be promoting the rights of disabled people.
- To be open about one's own motivations so that they do not influence the research.
- Always to allow the subjects to speak for themselves.
- To ensure that participants are co-researchers and allowed to set the agenda.
- To allow the disabled subjects to be involved in the analysis of the data.

The ones that were embraced were: to engage in critical disability research; and to give voice to the research subjects and take their views seriously. This latter one I particularly heeded, as Gerber asserts,

> the denial of a voice to disabled people has been over-determined in the case of those labelled 'mentally retarded' by our historically shifting criteria. In no other area has disabled people telling us about their lives seemed less diagnostically and therapeutically relevant. This label has carried

with it the understanding that individuals lack the power to learn or to reason. (1990, p. 4)

Next, to the injunction 'to celebrate subjectivity'. This issue of subjectivity is important as the social world is not objective but involves subjective meanings and experiences that participants construct in social contexts (Burgess 1993). Reason and Rowan (1981) argue for 'critical subjectivity' by which they mean that the validity of our encounter with experience is rooted in the critical and self-aware judgements of the researcher/s. Moreover, Steinar Kvale comments pointedly on the existence of 12 quite different dictionary definitions for the term 'objectivity', 'according to a definition of objectivity as intersubjective consensus, the lack of intersubjective agreement testifies to objectivity being a rather subjective notion' (1996, p. 64). Also, as a number of feminist writers have insisted objectivity is a fiction and Adrienne Rich expresses it pungently when she observes that 'objectivity is a word men use to describe their own subjectivity' (Morris 1992, p. 159).

To continue with the ground rules, the next is 'to ensure that the research leads to improvement for disabled people; to own up to a commitment to be promoting the rights of disabled people; and to be open about one's motivations so that they do not influence the research' (Moore, Beazley and Maelzer 1998). This last point is consonant with the feminist principles of standpoint epistemology. Moore et al. insist that disability research must be conducted within a social model of disability as they have found disastrous consequences from trying to work with people still wedded to a medical view (p. 63). One last point that can be complex to accommodate is always to allow subjects to speak for themselves. This is clearly an important issue as carers are likely to have their own agenda and there could be a clash of interests where carers see themselves as gatekeepers in institutional contexts. More discussion of this tenet will follow (at the end of this chapter) as we turn to the insights from researchers specifically working with people who do not have speech.

However, there are two ground rules that I was not able to

accommodate, for pragmatic rather than ideological reasons. These were: to ensure that participants are co-researchers and allowed to set the agenda as my research subjects were not intellectual wheelchair users, or visually impaired professors, but *intellectually* impaired people outside academia. In addition, this work was not initially envisaged as involving people with intellectual impairments. Finally, the disabled subjects to be involved in the analysis of the data. It might have been possible to get one or two of the subjects to comment on the data, but it was unlikely that they would be able to offer analysis (as the researcher would not have been confident to do that prior to attending a doctoral research methods course). I would argue that the requirement to do so could be a huge burden, amounting to oppressive practice coming from the opposite direction! Furthermore, the context in which I met these people was a recreational one and they were not likely to want to do any work for me.

Essentially what is argued for is 'a human rights perspective to be given to issues which shape disabled people's lives' (Moore et al. 1998, p. 13), and this I sought to heed as it fitted well with my values; with my concern for liberation of oppressed peoples and also to see issues of social justice addressed. What I hope to have demonstrated here is not so much a commitment to an emancipatory paradigm, which was not entirely possible, but an awareness of the value that the Disability Movement places on it and a respect for those perceptions and preferences.

Ethical Considerations

Ethics is always an important issue where research on human subjects is concerned. However, where the subjects are especially vulnerable this is even more the case. Ethics is a question of principled sensitivity to the rights of others and self, which consequently is likely to limit the choices researchers have in the way research is conducted. Bulmer (2001, p. 46) asserts that researchers must preserve the rights and integrity of their subjects as human beings, even at the expense of remaining ignorant of the matters that may be under review. In this section I will look at the question of who is entitled to do disability related research, issues of consent, the question of anonymity and confidentiality and finally reciprocity.

Who can research disability issues?

A central question for this subject area is, who can research disability issues? Moore et al. highlight the need to be

> critical of self in terms of values, presuppositions and practices [as] an essential part of developing a critical disability research process, particularly when reflections can be made in association with others and in relation to the voices of disabled people. (1998, p. 14)

There is one key ethical issue that relates to the substantive research area of disability. In some quarters it is argued that non-disabled people are less well placed to undertake research in this area. Ethically it is argued that there may be concerns about the 'control' of this area by non-disabled people. For example, according to Oliver (1992), Hirst and Baldwin (1994) and Gregory et al. (1996), much of the research that has been conducted by non-disabled researchers has been considered by disabled people to be either futile and/or to have negative consequences, undermining the agendas of disabled people. This has led to essentialist claims for the value of this type of research only being conducted by researchers with disabilities. However, Barnes points out that 'analytically the experience of impairment is not a unitary one'. And going further he notes,

> having an impairment does not automatically give someone an affinity with disabled people nor an inclination to do disability research ... Indeed I have met many people with impairments who are unsympathetic to the notion of disability as social oppression and many able-bodied people who are. (1992, p. 121)

Barnes also notes that matters of age, class, race, etc. are equally important to the issue of empathetic involvement. While there are ethical issues involved in who can speak for, or on behalf of, another person – ethical concerns of power, ownership and control – nevertheless while I recognized the need to remain vigilant in respect of these aspects in my research, my intention was to produce work that would be useful for church groups who work with/for people with disabilities.

Before moving on to look at consent, confidentiality and anonymity, and reciprocity, we should note the four main areas of concern highlighted by Diener and Crandall (1978) and alluded to by Bryman (2004):

- Whether there is harm to participants.
- Whether there is lack of informed consent.
- Whether there is an invasion of privacy.
- Whether deception is involved.

Harm to participants can mean anything from physical harm to loss of self-esteem, harm to participants' development or causing stress, or 'inducing subjects to perform reprehensible acts' as Diener and Crandall (1978, p. 19) articulate it. The other three categories are self-explanatory and the issue of consent is discussed here in some detail. Of course there can be some overlap of these categories.

Consent

It is axiomatic that a key ethical concern must be to ensure that, wherever possible, and as far as possible, participants should give their informed consent to the researcher (Bryman 2004). Furthermore, research participants must be aware that they have the right to withdraw from research contexts if they do not wish to participate (Bulmer 2001, p. 49). Moore et al. urge:

> It is important to recognize that when professionals in positions of power dictate to others that they will be involved in a project, and how, those who do become research participants may not have done so of their own accord. (1998, p. 23)

Jorgensen (1989) points out even when an overt strategy is employed not everyone knows about the true purpose of the research. This issue is complex for, in reality, overt and covert approaches can merge into one another, so that most observational work, as Adler argues is 'a delicate combination of overt and covert roles' (1987, p. 27). The issue of consent is similarly complex. In both places where I conducted research, consent had been negotiated with the gatekeepers (in this case the leaders), and as Fielding cautions 'you should allow for the possibility that the gatekeeper's permission may be given without the knowledge or consent of the others being studied' (2001, p. 150).

At both of my research sites verbal consent to conduct participant observation was given by the leaders, but a decision not to offer consent slips to the members was taken because of comprehension issues. The Social Science Research webpage on vulnerable adults and groups states 'in institutional settings, where conformity and compliance are rewarded, people may not feel they have a *real* choice'. It adds that 'refusals should not result in sanctions, adverse criticism or the loss of privileges', which historically has sometimes been the case. All in all, the issue of consent may not be an easy one to raise with people with learning disabilities. Withdrawal was not discussed but since it was a public setting and people came on a voluntary basis it could be argued that it was quite possible not to attend if anyone wanted to withdraw.

Consent was individually negotiated with interviewees as I often spoke to them during the participant observations times so I was able to ask them informally if they would be willing for me to interview them. I was in regular contact with the participants of the focus group who were members of the diocese and not from either of my research sites, so it was also quite natural to raise the question of doing an interview. Of the ten I invited to the focus group, only six were able to come which raises the possibility that some people used their right not to participate.

Confidentiality and anonymity

Although popularly used as synonyms, the two aspects of confidentiality and anonymity are distinct. Confidentiality refers to the attempt to remove from all data anything that could lead the subject to be identified, and anonymity, simply to the obscuring of the subject's or place's name. Berg cautions: 'in most qualitative research, however, because subjects are known to the investigators ... anonymity is virtually non-existent. Thus it is important to provide subjects with a high degree of confidentiality' (1989, p. 138).

It is common practice to use pseudonyms instead of actual names but it would be naive to assume that this is sufficient to obscure the identity of the person concerned as it is sometimes possible for participants at least, to identify individuals from other clues, in conjunction with place names (Gibbons 1975). In my study, place names were obscured as were the names of the churches I attended. I needed to protect the interests of all parties (Hammersley and Atkinson 1995, p. 66), including the leaders who I realized were anxious to safeguard their reputations.

Research with people with profound disabilities and no speech

Where research with people with profound intellectual disabilities is concerned, it seems that qualitative research and within that some form of inclusive research, that is, participatory or emancipatory, is becoming established as the preferred methodology, even though it has a fairly short history.

Reciprocity

In order for the research to be ethical, researchers sometimes perform services or make small payments in exchange
for information (Jorgensen 1989). My work did not so much
require me to make a contribution for information so much
as to play my part in all the work involved in these ministries.
Jorgensen says, 'morally responsible participant observation
requires that you be alert to ways of providing something of
value in exchange for what you get' (1989, p. 72).

At the other site, partly to make a contribution and partly to
help build my relationship with the members of the Kingsway
group, I made popcorn with them, having previously established that they liked it. One group member started to call
me 'the popcorn lady' which pleased me, as Johnson (1975)
reminds that data is improved where good field relationships
are established and sustained.

In this section we have considered issues around conducting disability research. I have flagged some possible difficulties
when the research subjects have intellectual impairments,
based on my own work. We now enter the debate more deeply
drawing on recent work which seeks to find suitable research
methods for people with profound disabilities including those
who may not have speech.

The approach of Swinton, Mowat and Baines at the University of Aberdeen

In their article 'Whose Story Am I? Describing Profound
Intellectual Disability in the Kingdom of God', John Swinton
(University of Aberdeen), with Harriet Mowat and Susannah
Baines, explain how their university has developed a unique
programme of action-orientated research that explores the
role of spirituality in the lives of people with intellectual
abilities. The title itself raises an interesting angle. Swinton
expounds: 'All of us live in a complex matrix of narratives and
counternarratives that merge together, sometimes coherently,

sometimes quite incoherently, to give us a sense of who we are and why we are in the world' (2011, p. 6). Thus narratives and counternarratives are at the heart of this research.

Returning to methodological matters, the centre's projects all hold two dimensions in common. First, there is an emphasis on participation, enabling people with intellectual impairments to be fully involved in the entire research process from design through to analysis. Second, all projects are action-orientated with a view to generating new knowledge that can transform practice (Swinton 2011, p. 6).

The projects focus on reflecting theologically on the real lives of people with profound intellectual disabilities with high support needs (one of whom is Brian). The work was conducted over an 18-month period with the subjects and their families, care takers and support workers. The article offers a discussion of what took place and the insights recorded. Swinton suggests,

> perhaps the best way to view what this discussion offers is to see it as a series of extended meditations on the lives of some real people and the issues that they bring to the table as theological conversations develop. As we reflect together on their experiences, so we will find ourselves challenged to rethink some important theological questions and perhaps even to change. (2011, p. 6)

This research also makes use of a theory known as positioning theory (Romme Harré 1999) which is best understood in contrast to role theory. Roles tend to describe typical positions such as grandfather, sister, chef, etc. Yet roles tell us very little about the actual experience of living in a particular role whereas 'positioning theory offers a more dynamic perspective than role theory, focusing on the special position of a particular individual within an encounter' (2011, p. 7). It is from using this framework that the researchers claim some key insights. Regarding the interview with Brian's mother, the researchers note, what we see in Brian's mother's statement is her positioning him within their relationship in a quite specific way. Cultural narratives may commonly position Brian as disabled, unable to communicate, a tragic figure; his mother linguistically positions him as 'a good person' and in so doing offers a simple but powerful *counternarrative* [own emphasis] that gives Brian a quite different story. Despite his disability, despite the apparent negativity of his situation, Brian's mother tells a story that positions him as a good person – just as he is. (2011, p. 8)

The work of Jill Harshaw at Belfast Bible College

Jill Harshaw, an academic with great respect for Swinton, and mother of a profoundly disabled daughter with no speech, raises some concerns here. She does not dispute the value of Brian's mother being able to talk at length about her son, and how she sees his life but she raises the critical question of whether this is Brian's new narrative or simply his mother's. Forcefully she asserts: 'Surely, we do not know what Brian feels or believes or would like to say about himself for he cannot tell us' (2016, p. 71–2). We will hear more of Harshaw's concerns about the trend to use qualitative research methods with subjects who lack speech at the end of this chapter. Returning now to the work of Swinton, Mowat and Baines, their research also reveals some fascinating points about the nature of spirituality. Mary is a young woman with profound intellectual disabilities. She has cerebral palsy, cannot speak and is blind. Mary has been part of the Quaker community since birth. Quakers place a lot of importance on silence. The researchers note that Mary tends to shout noisily with intermittent wails, yet as the community moves into silence Mary also mirrors their silence. Swinton et al. comment:

Her spirituality is being formed and held by her participation in the community. Mary's spirituality is not simply within her. It is something she shares in; it is an experience that rises beyond her; an experience that happens in the space between the members of the community: the space of meeting. She is dependent on her community for her spiritual experience. If that is the case, then Mary's spirituality is a corporate rather than a personal concept and experience. (2011, p. 14)

Having made this observation about Mary the writers go on to question whether if this is so for Mary might it not equally apply to the rest of us. They then appeal to 1 Corinthians 3.16 in support of such a view, where Paul asserts: 'Don't you know that you yourselves are God's temple and that God's Spirit lives among you?'

Swinton et al. conclude:

If then Jesus is, in whatever sense, within us, and if our relationships are the place where we learn what love looks and feels like, then Christian friendships are a place where we physically encounter God. That being so, Mary's relationships within her community not only hold and sustain her spirituality (and she theirs) they are also the place where she encounters God in tangible ways. (2011, p. 15)

Solitude and community

Harshaw also takes issue with this interpretation for, while accepting the truth of it, she disputes that it tells the whole story: 'The ancient spiritual disciplines of solitude and community emphasize the importance of experiencing God both alone and together' (2016, p. 82). She also points out the danger of Mary's spiritual life being dependent on a community that could move on and leave Mary bereft of her spiritual life.

What Swinton's research and perspective highlights is that people with profound learning disabilities are also recipients of God's love and grace. So much thinking in the church concerning disability seems to focus on making *them* like *us*. A friend told me of a ministry in her church where people's upper limbs were manipulated with scarves so it looked like they could raise their arms. She told me as if it were an enlightened and groundbreaking move!

John Swinton brings some welcome corrective to this sort of perspective as he points to a relationship of mutuality and reception. In Hans Reinders' collection of essays *The Paradox of Disability* (2010), we find a heart-warming essay called 'Known by God' in which Swinton fleshes out his life-affirming perspective.

In his early days as a nurse and later as a mental health chaplain, Swinton was always passionate about the prospect of all people having a relationship with God. However, as he dipped into the disability literature the grounds for his excitement evaporated. He quotes the Birchenalls who though writing in the late 1980s, depict a worldview, the legacy of which Swinton believes is still with us. The Birchenalls raise doubts over the capacity for people with profound disabilities to reason and therefore to process doubts and arrive at a point of faith. Further they state:

> Such an existence gives no real opportunity for inner spiritual growth, or the nourishment of the human spirit, both of which are important when coming to terms with the meaning of Christianity. (1986, p. 75)

Swinton rightly objects that the emphasis here is on knowing *about* God rather than *being known* by God. The concept of faith is purely an intellectual one that is necessarily exclusive. Swinton urges that

> faith itself is not a human achievement but a grace-full gift … if the theological dynamic begins and ends in divine grace and human reception then the situation of people with profound intellectual disabilities begins to look quite different … viewed in this way, the issue is not really one of intellect versus experience, but activism versus reception. (2010, p. 144)

Contemplative spirituality and a God beyond words

Taking us into the arena of contemplative prayer and experience foregrounds the limitation imposed by the intellect rather than a lack of intellectual capacity. Thomas Merton taught that contemplation led to a supernatural knowledge of God. Towards the end of his life Karl Rahner spoke compellingly about the immediacy and inclusivity of God's presence (1982, p. 374ff.) 'I have experienced God directly ... I have experienced God himself, not human words about him. This experience is not barred to anyone.'

Swinton concludes:

> the contemplative tradition brings us clearly and gently into the knowledge that all we have is gift, and that no matter how hard we strive to get closer to God, in the end it is he who comes to us and not the other way around. (2010, p. 145)

And if the limits of intellect have been challenged here now the human capacity for any person to fully know God is also thoroughly contested. Referring to the cataphatic and the apophatic theological traditions Swinton reminds us:

> The human encounter with God sits in that strange space between knowing and not knowing: revelation and hiddenness. The recognition of the great mystery and the deep sense of unknowability does not mean that we can know nothing of God, only that what we know is always tentative and partial. (2010, p. 147)

Given the universality of this human position Swinton suggests that our encounter with people with profound disabilities may be uncomfortable as it reminds us of truths that have become unpopular in our culture; namely that progress and activism are not all that counts.

This is not a detached, mystical spirituality but one that also sees the importance of God being 'embodied in faithful people', and here Swinton argues for a shift in the relationship between people with profound disabilities and the rest of the Body of Christ to one of mutuality, with each learning and receiving from the other.

Ultimately Swinton hopes to turn our practices towards what he calls 'faithful and transformative' discipleship.

> It is as we recognize the poverty of our own spirits and learn to accept the ministry of Jesus as it comes to us in the stranger that we all discover that God's actions precede our loving acts of response. It's all gift. (2010, p. 151)

An example of how this might look is offered here. A friend of mine was organizing the music for a community meal in her town. When she arrived everyone seemed to have found a place to sit and she felt excluded. As she was fiddling with the speakers she felt a tap on her shoulder and turned round to the welcoming smile of a woman with profound learning disabilities and no speech whose parents she knew a little. This woman, who she might wrongly have assumed she could receive nothing from, had made her feel so welcome. My friend told me this story as she said it was her first instance of the sort of thing I had been talking about since starting my work on disability. I have noted other instances of people with pro-found learning disabilities showing empathetic concern for others that the rest of the congregation had not picked up on. I wonder if it is because most of us so-called able people are too self-absorbed/self-important to really notice anyone else.

The many concepts unpacked in Swinton's 'Known by God' (Reinders 2010) are key to a fresh understanding of the place of people with profound disabilities in the church today. Never-theless we must return to some of Harshaw's concerns about the alleged findings of Swinton's research with people who lack speech.

Harshaw's reservations are important to voice as she is a qualitative researcher and a practical theologian (teaching both at Queens in Belfast and Belfast Bible College) and it could be said that her motivations are similar to Swinton's in that they both desire full inclusion of people with profound disabilities in the church. So her concern here is not with intentions but with rigour. It might be fair to say that her concern is that Swinton et al. are skating on thin ice, especially in regard to using data from close others including observer/interpreters which she fears can lead to lack of credibility. She wonders if their desire for convincing data could be driven by an over-defensive stance, despite laudable motivations, and cautions:

> when qualitative research is used inappropriately with those who cannot speak for themselves, the theological knowledge which is the purported outcome is less than sustainable, and that in seeking to achieve valuable insight into the spiritual lives of people with profound intellectual disabilities, this failed methodology results in potentially unreliable and detri-mental conclusions. (2016, p. 79)

A key concern here is the lack of acknowledgement of degree where people with profound learning disabilities are con-cerned. She argues for the necessary differentiation between those whose cognitive understanding enables them to grasp the questions clearly and whose linguistic capabilities allow for authentic self-expression in response and those who are not so able. Potently she concludes: 'Once again in qualitative research as in disability studies in general, "impairment does matter"' (p. 76).

The research work of Melanie Nind for the Economic and Social Research Council

These concerns raised by Harshaw are all the more important as we turn to the conclusions of Melanie Nind who produced a review paper for the ESRC on the methodological challenges of using qualitative research with people with learning, com-municative and other disabilities and assumes the capacity for speech and therefore does not acknowledge any of these reser-vations for using qualitative research methods with subjects who do not have speech.

Nind concludes:

> Conducting qualitative research with people with learning/communication difficulties is challenging but achievable. This synthesis of research literature by academics and researchers with learning disabilities shows how shared knowledge in relation to addressing the challenges is developing. This is a rapidly developing field and a couple of decades ago the practical guidance contained in this review would not have been available. The synthesis shows how the practical, political and ethical challenges and sensitivities are interwoven with each other and across all stages of the research process. These challenges are being taken up now, not just by the pioneers in the field but by a whole raft of researchers in a range of disciplines who would no longer consider conducting research on people with learning and communication difficulties without, first and foremost, addressing them as human beings with something to say that is worth hearing. (2008, p. 16)

Points for Discussion and/or Reflection

Returning to your first encounter with disability,

1 What model of disability do you think you had internalized to feel the way you did?
2 Would a different model have enabled you to feel differently or even see in a more positive light?

References

Adler, P. A. and Adler, P. (1987), *Membership Rites in Field Research*, Newbury Park: Sage.
Aspis, S. (1999), *Reclaiming the Social Model of Disability*, London: BSA Conference, paper: GLAD.

Barnes, C. (1992), 'Qualitative research: valuable or irrelevant', *Disability, Handicap and Society*, 7/2, pp. 115–23.

Barton, L. (ed.) (1996), *Disability and Society: Emerging issues and insights*, London: Longman.

Berg, B. (1989), *Qualitative Research Methods for the Social Sciences*, Massachusetts: Allyn & Bacon.

Birchenall, P. and Birchenall, M. (1986), 'Caring for mentally handicapped people in the community and the church', *The Professional Nurse* 1.6, pp. 150ff.

Brett. J. (2002), 'The Experience of Disability from the Perspective of Parents of Children with Profound Impairment: Is it time for an alternative model of disability?', *Disability & Society* 17(7), pp. 825–43

Bryman, A. (2004), *Social Research Methods*, Oxford: Oxford University Press.

Bulmer, P. (2001), 'Social measurement. What stands in its way?' *Social Research* 68(2), pp. 455–80.

Burgess, R. (1993), *In the Field: An Introduction to Field Research*, London: Routledge.

Bury, M. B. (1996), 'Defining and researching disability: Challenges and responses', in Barnes, C. and Mercer, G. (eds), *Exploring the divide: Illness and disability*, Leeds: The Disability Press, pp. 83–105.

Cameron, D. (1988), *The Feminist Critique of Language*, Abingdon: Routledge.

Campbell, J. (2002), 'Valuing diversity: the disability agenda – we've only just begun', *Disability & Society* 17/(4), pp. 471–8.

Corker, M. (1999), *Disability Discourse: Disability Human Rights and Society*, Buckingham: Open University.

Creamer, D. (1998), *Disability and Christian Theology: Embodied Limits and Constructive Possibilities*, Oxford: Oxford University Press.

Cresswell, J. W. (2007), *Qualitative Enquiry and Research Design*, London: Sage.

De Jong, G. (1979), *The Movement for Independent Living: Origins, ideology and implications for disability research*, Michigan: University Center for Rehabilitation.

Diener, E. and Crandall, R. (1978), *Ethics in Social and Behavioural Research*, Chicago: University of Chicago Press.

Eiesland, N. and Saliers, D. (eds) (1998), *Human Disability and the Service of God*, Nashville: Abingdon Press.

Fielding, N. (2001), 'On the Compatibility of Qualitative and Quantitative Research Methods', *The Forum: Qualitative Social Research*, vol. 2(1).

Fielding, N. (2001) (ed.), *Researching Social Life* (2nd edn), London and Thousand Oaks, CA: Sage.

Fine, M. (1990), 'The "public" in public schools: The construction/ constriction of moral communities', *Journal of Social issues* 46(1).

Finkelstein, V. (1981), 'To Deny or not to Deny Disability', in Brechin, A., Liddiard, P. and Swain, J. (eds), *Handicap in a Social World*, Sevenoaks: Hodder & Stoughton, and Milton Keynes: The Open University, pp. 34–6.

Freire, P. (1970), *Pedagogy of the Oppressed*, New York: Continuum Publishing Company.

Geertz, C. (1973), *The Interpretation of Cultures*, New York: Basic Books.

Gerber, D. (1990) 'Listening to Disabled People: The problem of voice and authority', in Edgerton, R., 'The Cloak of Competence', *Disability, Handicap and Society* 5(1), pp. 3–22.

Gibbons, D. (1975), 'Unidentified research sites and fictitious names', *American Sociologist* 10, pp. 32–6.

Gilbert, N. (2001), *Resourcing Social Life* (2nd edn), Newbury Park, CA: Sage.

Gregory, S., Bishop, J. and Sheldon, L. (1996), *Deaf Young People and Their Families: Developing understanding*, Cambridge: Cambridge University Press.

Hahn, H. (1986), 'Public support for rehabilitation programs: The analysis of US disability policy', *Disability, Handicap and Society* 1(2), pp. 121–38.

Hammersley, M. and Atkinson, P. (1995), *Ethnography: Principles in practice* (2nd edn), London and New York: Routledge.

Harré, R. (1999), *Recent Advances in Positioning Theory*, ResearchGate.

Harshaw, J. (2016), *God Beyond Words*, London: Jessica Kingsley.

Hirst, M. and Baldwin, S. (1994), *Unequal Opportunities: Growing up disabled*, Social Policy Research Unit, London: HMSO.

Johnson, J. M. (1975), *Doing Field Research*, New York: Free Press.

Jorgensen, D. (1989), *Participant Observation*, London, New Delhi: Sage.

Kvale, S. (1996), *InterViews: An introduction to qualitative research interviewing*, Thousand Oaks: Sage.

McCloughry, R. and Morris, W. (2002), *Making a world of Difference*, London: SPCK.

Miller, E. J. and Gwynne, G. V. (1972), *A life apart*, London: Tavistock.

Moore, M., Beazley, S. and Maelzer, J. (eds) (1998), *Researching Disability Issues*, Milton Keynes: Open University Press.

Morris, J. (1992), 'Personal and Political: a feminist perspective on researching physical disability', *Disability, Handicap and Society*, 7(2), pp. 157–66.

Nind, M. (2008), 'Conducting Qualitative research with people with learning, communication and other disabilities: Methodological challenges', ESRC report, National Centre for Research Methods Review Paper.

Oliver, M. (1983), *Social work with disabled people*, London: Macmillan.

Oliver, M. (1992), 'Changing the social relations of research production?' *Disability, Handicap and Society* 7(2) 101, p. 14

Pfeiffer, D. (1995), 'The Disability Movement and its History', first published as 'Hip Crip 101', *Mainstream: Magazine of the Able-Disabled*, December–January 1994–95.

Rahner, K. (1982), *Theological Investigations*, New York: Crossroads.

Reason, P. and Rowan, J. (eds) (1981), *Human Inquiry: A sourcebook of new Paradigm research*, New York: John Wiley & Sons.

Reindal, S. (2008), 'A Social Relational Model of Disability: A theoretical framework for Special Needs Education', *European Journal of Special Needs Education* 23(2), pp. 135–46.

Reinders, H. (2010) (ed.), *The Paradox of Disability*, Grand Rapids: Eerdmanns.

Rieser, R. and Mason, M. (1990), *Disability equality in the classroom: A human rights issue* (2nd edn), London.

Rieser, R. and Mason, M. (1990), *Disability in the Classroom: A Human Rights Issue*, London: [no further info.]

Shakespeare, R. (2006), *Disability Rights and Wrongs*, Routledge: London.

Swinton, J. (2011) 'Who is the God we worship? Theologies of disability: challenges and new possibilities', Research report, School of divinity, history and philosophy, Kings College, Aberdeen.

Swinton, J., Mowat, H. and Baines. S. (2011), 'Whose Story Am I? Redescribing profound intellectual disability in the kingdom of God. *Journal of religion, disability and Health* 15:1, 5–19.

Swinton, J. and Mowat, H. (2016), *Practical Theology and Qualitative Research* (2nd edn), London: SCM Press.

Thomas, C. (1999), *Female Forms: experiencing and understanding disability*, Buckingham: Open University Press.

Usher, R. and Edwards, R. (1994), *Postmodernism and Education*, London: Routledge.

Yong, A. (2007), *Theology and Down Syndrome: Reimagining Disability in Late Modernity*, Texas: Baylor University Press.

Zarb, G. (1992), 'Changing the relations of disability research', *Disability Handicap & Society*, 7(2), pp. 125–38

Summary

In this chapter we have explored the major models of disability as recognized in disability studies. First we looked at the medical model, which was the dominant one until recently, then the social model, which has largely displaced it, was explored including some criticisms of it. Four, further, lesser models are explored, which can be charted somewhere on the spectrum between medical and social. Having laid this conceptual foundation we moved on to explore suitable models for conducting disability research. Ethical considerations were explored here too. In considering critical disability research, the author offered some discussion as related to her own research work with subjects who have learning disabilities and some limitations she found in applying the tenets of critical disability research to this constituency. Discussion then moved on to the issue of suitable research methodology for subjects with profound learning disabilities who also lack speech, and here we entered a new yet already contested domain.

3

Being Human and Personhood

Who is Fully Human?

It has been said that any enquiry into what makes us human has an underlying agenda and such concepts are often used for polemical and institutional uses. Feminist writer, Naomi Scheman, drawing on her dual experience as lesbian Jew, gives us a pungent and insightful explanation. I quote her here in full.

Twentieth century liberatory activism and theorizing have lived with and on the tension between two visions. For one the goal is to secure for the marginalized and oppressed the relief from burdens and the access to benefits reserved for the privileged, including the benefits of being thought by others and oneself to be at the centre of one's society's views of what it is to be fully human. For the other the goal is to disrupt those views and the models of privileged selfhood that they underwrite – to claim not the right to be, in those terms, fully human but, rather, the right to be free of a stigmatizing, normalizing, apparatus to which one would not choose to conform even if one were allowed or encouraged to do so. (1997, p. 124)

The Limits Model of Disability

Focusing on the reality of our human embodiment, Deborah Creamer posits the Limits Model of Disability. In *Christian Theology and Disability* she argues for a constructive marriage

of theology and disability studies. This now takes us beyond
the purely secular models we examined in Chapter 2. Creamer's
model is drawn from disability studies, theology, biblical
thought, anthropology and feminism and she makes three
broad claims about limitation per se. Crucially she sees limits
as a central aspect of the human condition and an inevitable
consequence of human existence. Further she sees them as positive and not negative. The limits model enables her to bypass
oppressive concepts of 'normal' and 'abnormal'. Building on
the foundation of inherent limits to the human condition she
proposes that disability be the starting point for a consideration of what being human means. It is a thoroughly inclusive
approach as all human beings find themselves somewhere on
the spectrum of limitation though that may vary from human
to human and vary across the lifespan of any given individual.
Let us now look at what our society regards as normal for
human beings.

The Concept of Normality

The concept of 'normality' is highly contentious as it is seen to
be in opposition to diversity. Normal is a statistical construction derived from an average of the population, for example if
50 per cent of the sample are 20 stone but the other 50 per cent
are 8 stone the norm would be set as 14 stone even if none of the
subjects was that actual weight. This construct was epitomized
in the introduction of the bell curve. So in fact there may be
no one individual who meets this standard. This lack of reality
regarding human embodiment leads to a hopeless striving for
many simply to conform to set standards that are unattainable
on account of being conceived from a fictitious idealism. Blind
theologian John Hull raises issues with the concept of normal
being uniform. He particularly objects to the image of God in
the Bible being unitary rather than poly-anthropomorphic:

> Normality must become inclusive. This will lead us into
> a critique of other forms of exclusion, including the most

powerful of all, the exclusion of the poor by the rich. In some such way, a theology of blindness will offer a utopian promise of universal liberation. (2013, p. 41)

Where the word 'normalization' appears in the disability literature, it has a thoroughly different and positive meaning. It refers to the right of disabled people to all the same things in life that constitute a 'normal' life, for example, employment, independent living, sexual relationships, parenthood and so on.

In *Vulnerable Communion* (2008) Reynolds points out how society has established a 'cult of normalcy' which becomes a lens through which all of life is viewed. From that vantage point disability becomes something that needs changing. As we have seen 'normal' is a slippery concept. However, if we challenge the status quo then it is not disability but the status quo which needs transformation. Humans have limits and are vulnerable beings needing relationships of interdependence and not fierce independence as valued in western society. Unlike Enlightenment conceptions of the Self, which rejected the notion of embodiment for its implication of fragility and likely dissolution; the decentred subject need not fear embodiment.

The Individual or Self

We will now take one step further and introduce the concept of the individual or Self and then move on to personhood. Briefly, the individual or the Self has been of central importance in western culture as it sits at the intersection of ethics, metaphysics and epistemology. Feminist writers take issue with the western assumption that selves are discreet beings, cleanly divided from their surroundings. Keller shows how language itself underscores this point. 'The Latin for self is *se* meaning "on one's own", yields with *parare* "to prepare" the verb to separate. For our culture it is separation that prepares the way to selfhood' (Keller 1986, p. 1). Keller rejects this view which Freudian psychology has strengthened: she finds more sympathy with a Jungian approach which is more integrationist.

Women's experience articulates psychological, sociological and philosophical insights which are broadly relational in character. For example, the social-psychologist, Nancy Chodorow argued that boys develop through separation, whereas girls develop through relationality and connection: 'The basic feminine self is connected to the world, the basic masculine sense is separate' (1999, p. 14).

Personhood

'Person' comes from the Latin for a mask and Jung talks of the persona as does Erving Goffman: it is our interface with society. As such it does not denote anything ontological, coming from the ancient theatre, persona denoting an 'appearance' as one actor may appear in several distinct and separate roles. On this basis a human being may be nothing more than a complex set of shifting facades. So we must dig deeper since we are made in the image of God who has actual ontological existence.

Sociologist/anthropologist Marcel Mauss writing on sociology and psychology advances the view that the notion of a person owes its metaphysical foundation to Christianity (1979, p. 87). The concept of person came to light during the defence of the Trinity by the Desert Fathers in the early third century. The Latin-speaking church used the term 'persona', suggesting that the person is an 'agent'. However, the Greek-speaking church spoke of a *hypostasis* (which literally means substance but could be usefully translated as 'subject') for this implies a reality underlying all that a person presents. This lack of ontological reality meant that the Fathers refused to use the Greek term *prosopon* for the persons of the Trinity as it would have rendered God as three masks with a true substance elsewhere.

The Orthodox bishop John Zizoulas argues that an effect of the Fall is that in the dislocation of the intimate relationship between humankind and God, humans cease to be full persons and become mere individuals. So we become individuals by virtue of our human birth alone but only persons by participating in the divine personhood through the new birth. Thus the concept of person is found only in God as it implies a movement towards communion which transcends the boundaries of the Self.

Catholic, feminist theologian Mary Grey notes that the concept of 'existential estrangement' so beloved of Sartre and others, is crucially a problem of the 'disengaged I'. For Grey 'the connected Self knows no existential estrangement' (1993, p. 80).

Moral and political philosophers have tended to take the able-bodied, healthy adult as the paradigmatic person and have failed to pay attention to human vulnerability and disability as part of the human condition. Susan Wendell notes that our culture rejects any concept of the 'independent' individual as being more fully human and advances the self-deception that we are not all thoroughly dependent on one another. In our attempt to consider what constitutes a person we extend the paradigm to embrace those who are other than 'able-bodied, adults'. Essentially all those who are 'made in the image of God' qualify to be considered as persons. It used to be that cognitive abilities were privileged so that those who could reason were deemed full humans. Much thinking has moved on to social and relational capacities, but Jill Harshaw argues that can still leave out those who have profound disabilities who may also lack speech. She argues that if not all of us are deemed made in the image of God then that challenges God's ability of self-revelation. As we have seen, John Swinton's work 'Known by God' addresses this issue.

Theological anthropology takes us further than sociology in a discussion of personhood

Insights from Theological Anthropology

There will be three prongs to our enquiry into theological anthropology. First, since we are made in the image of the triune God, we can find an examination of what the Trinity means instructive to the way we are designed to be. Second, we will look at the two-sex creation which also reflects the imago

Dei. Finally, the life of Jesus Christ as the perfect Son of God. East and West have understood the Trinity in different terms although the eastern view taken from the Cappadocian Fathers has drawn increasing interest in the West in the present day. In fact, the concept of the Trinity has been enjoying something of a revival having been very out of vogue during recent decades. Broadly, the western view taken from Augustine is seen as a 'psychological' view based on a triadic human psychology, whereas the eastern view is strongly social and relational. Martin Buber puts it: 'All real living is meeting' (1958, p. 11).

McFayden is excellent here on his understanding of the Genesis paradigm – largely in so wisely and carefully avoiding many pitfalls as he unpacks what it does and indeed does not denote. As with the Trinity, so the male–female one flesh relationship is completely inclusive, according to McFayden. Defining the 'one flesh' relationship outside the parameters of heterosexual marriage, McFayden skilfully embraces all humanity in its rich diversity. The author shows us the breadth of his awareness of the potential for exclusion in other interpretations.

> Marriage and sexual intercourse are not equivalent terms for the paradigm of 'male' and 'female'. If they were, then the corresponding understanding of human nature would be exclusivist. It would place those male–female relations in which neither marriage nor coitus is a part into a subordinate position and the humanity of all those unable or choosing not to enter such relations in question. The elderly, the impotent, the widowed, the celibate, the hermaphrodite, the transsexual, the deformed and handicapped [sic] and the homosexual would have their humanity and the humanity of their inter-relationships denied them. The creation narratives do afford some special status to procreative, and therefore potent, heterosexual relations; however, procreation is construed as a blessing which is bestowed not primarily on individuals but on the species so that it can continue through generation. In short, this way of understanding the image provides no basis for the exclusion of the homosexual, the single and the variously infertile from the image (1990, p. 38).

It should be noted that some disabled people resent a common assumption that because they are disabled they are not capable of full sexual relations. It is important to include this here simply to acknowledge that for some that even if this is so, they are not excluded from the imago Dei as set forth in the Genesis account.

Looking at the Genesis account of the rest of creation Balkan theologian, Miroslav Volf draws out an important principle. He points out that creation includes 'separating-and-binding' rather than simply 'separating' suggesting that 'identity' includes connection, difference and heterogeneity. The human self is formed not through a simple rejection of the other but through a complex process of 'taking in' and 'keeping out'.

> We are who we are because we are both separate and connected, both distinct and related; the boundaries that mark our identities are both barriers and bridges. (1996, p. 66)

Finally, we will consider Christ in his incarnation as the paradigm of what it means to be a person. Volf states:

> In Christ human personhood became historical reality. Christ is the opposite of an individual; he is the person *par excellence*, since his identity is constituted by a twofold relation, namely, through his relationship as Son to the Father and as head to his body. (1998, p. 84)

William Placher in *Narratives of a Vulnerable God: Christ, theology and scripture*, challenges the popular notion held by those who are attracted to the idea of God and also those who are not, that they have a view of God centred on power. In contrast Placher underlines the fact that the God of the Bible is love, and love involves risk, and vulnerability to risk even leads to great suffering. God as revealed in Jesus welcomes outcasts into the Kingdom and opens up relationships beyond the accepted social boundaries.

We see then that we are persons as we participate in the life of the triune God, which is characterized by a transcendence beyond the self always reaching out to the other in love. Being in God's image (as seen in the life of Christ) is characterized by giving and vulnerable risk-taking rather than by great acts of power and ego-enhancing prestige.

The nature of persons in God reveals that, in contradiction to the Enlightenment view, what matters is not so much the ego reflecting upon itself, but a self-transcendence in communication with others, especially in the movement of love. The person lives from openness beyond itself to others, relationship being the central point.

In keeping with the argument so far, the underlying ethos of *God Beyond Words* is, as Harshaw states, 'that neither cognitive impairment nor any other aspect of the human experience has any power whatsoever to undermine the theological foundation of human personhood' (2016, p. 13). Harshaw also points out that people with profound disabilities are called 'to live out their vocation as beloved', thus challenging the values of western materialist culture.

The journey into God is the same for all, as Yale academic Erin Staley points out: 'It is a journey in which love subsumes intellect, higher forms of knowing include lower forms, and grace alone empowers the final movement from intellect to love' (2012, p. 386).

A Trinitarian Model of Disability

The Trinitarian model of disability, as set out by the Ukrainian Tataryns takes the insights of the social model of disability as axiomatic, in particular its uncovering of the disabling nature of our society, but its main contribution is that it is a fully inclusive model regardless of the passing trends in secular society. The theological paradigm is rooted in our Christian heritage, which sees the Creator as united in diversity within the Holy Trinity, thus opening us a space for all to be welcomed within the Trinitarian community of the church. As such this community creates sanctuary from the prevailing norms/prejudices of society at large. All persons are created in the image of God, a fact that confers dignity on each and every person. It also lays emphasis on the vital human need for relationship. Mark's Gospel constantly foregrounds events where disabled individuals, marginalized by their communities are embraced by the loving attention of Jesus who restores them to the circle of fellowship within their community (Tataryn 2013, p. 42). So community is fulfilled in the hospitality that resides at its core. This hospitality welcomes the stranger as if welcoming Christ himself and thus the stranger is seen as a blessing moving the community towards a greater and fuller expression of what it is to be truly human.

Tataryn states:

> Essentially, 'brokenness' is not diminishment; it is salvific and fundamental to the human–divine relationship, to the newly established koinonia. The true human community is built upon the one whose body was broken for the sake of love. To be in relationship with God then is to recognize one's brokenness and to share in the community of solidarity created by Christ's cross. (2013, p. 50)

Trinitarian Christianity presents a God who embraces humanity in its rich diversity and is able to radically transform persons so that they too can embrace each other in their manifold differences.

Personhood and the Church

Two important points are to be made from what has been said. First, that the church should reflect what we know to be true about God's nature and personhood and as such draw to him. 'Only unity in multiplicity can claim to correspond to God' (Volf 1998, p. 193), and therefore only a demonstration of multiplicity in unity will be adequate to set forth the life of God in the community of believers. Tataryn says: 'Living as trinity, we too, create miracles in our relationships with one another, rejecting social hierarchies and enveloping each other in love' (2013, p. 101). The concept of personhood has a strong eschatological dimension and as such the church should provide a taste of what is to come, including the reality of Galatians 3, equality of gender, race, economic status, and much more. Clearly this is not always the case but is a standard we must seek to attain in order to live out the dignity and blessing of the gospel of Jesus Christ.

Points for Discussion and/or Reflection

1 What do you think or feel about the concept of 'normality'? Have you ever felt excluded from that category?
2 What other groups of people may feel excluded from that definition in the church or just in society at large?
3 What is your response to the two new models of disability here propounded by Deborah Creamer (limits model) and the Tataryns (Trinitarian model)?

References

Buber, M. (1958) (2nd edn), *I and Thou*, trans. Ronald. G. Smith, Edinburgh: T & T Clark.

Chodorow, N. (1999), *The Reproduction of Mothering*, California: University of California Press.

Creamer, D. (2008), *Christian Theology and Disability: Embodied Limits, Constructive Possibilities*, Oxford: OUP.

Grey, M. (1993), *The Wisdom of Fools*, London: SPCK.

Hull, J. (2003), 'A spirituality of Disability: The Christian Heritage as both Problem and Potential', *Studies in Christian Ethics* vol. 16(2), pp. 21–35.

Hull, J. (2013), *The Tactile Heart*, London: SCM Press.

Harshaw, J. (2016), *God Beyond Words*, London: Jessica Kingsley.

Keller, C. (1986), *From a broken web*, Boston: Beacon Press.

Mauss, M. (1979), *Sociology and Psychology*, London: Routledge & Kegan Paul.

McFayden, A. (1990), *The call to personhood*, Cambridge: Cambridge University Press.

Placher, W. (1994), *Narratives of a Vulnerable God: Christ, theology and scripture*, Louisville Kentucky: Westminster John Knox Press.

Reynolds, T. (2008), *Vulnerable Communion*, Michegan: Brazos Press.

Scheman, N. (1997), 'Queering the Centre by centering the Queer', in Meyers, D. T., *Feminists rethink the Self*, Oxford: Westview Press, pp. 124–6.

Staley, E. (2012) 'Intellectual disability and mystical unknowing; contemporary insights from sources', *Modern Theology* 28:3, pp. 385–401.

Tataryn, M. and Trunchan-Tataryn, M. (2013), *Discovering Trinity in Disability*, New York, Orbis Books.

Volf, M. (1996), *Exclusion and Embrace*, Nashville: Abingdon Press.

Volf, M. (1998), *After our likeness: The Church as the image of the trinity*, Grand Rapids: Eerdmanns.

Wendell, S. (1996), *The Rejected Body*, New York and London: Routledge.

Summary

In this chapter we have explored what it means to be fully human and Creamer's limits model of disability was introduced. The contentious issue of normality was highlighted in the context of being human. Varying concepts of the individual, the Self and a person were then discussed. In order to open out the subject of personhood, a theological exploration was pursued, and from this the Trinitarian model of disability (Tataryns) was advanced. Insights were gleaned from theological anthropology. Finally we focused on the church and what it is intended to reveal of personhood and the divine.

4

Further Elements in a Constructive Theology of Disability

Before reading this chapter make a few notes on how you account for suffering in the world today.

Sadly, it still seems to be the case that in many places the existence of disability is regarded through the lens of some folkloric belief system, or more recently in the West through the health and wealth lens of the prosperity gospel. These lenses cause people with disabilities to be regarded with suspicion in much the same way as Job's friends viewed him once disaster had struck his life. It could be argued that it is bad enough when life does not turn out as expected without being 'demonized/victimized' for it. Swinton points out a surprising benefit of the medical model in this context. Here some parents have been treated with suspicion on account of their son not being healed from cerebral palsy:

> It is interesting to note that in this story it is the theological narrative that becomes profoundly negative and problematic within the lives of this family. It is the medical narrative that is the counternarrative that when told allieviates guilt, offers a very different definition of the situation and enables people to see things quite differently. (Swinton et al. 2011, p. 10)

More narratives about this are included in Chapter 6 where we look at tensions between the institutional church and the gospel.

Within the human psyche there is a very strong drive to understand life so that a really poor explanation can sometimes be embraced in favour of confronting the mystery to which we have no answer and thus no formulas to protect ourselves from the same fate. There are many people within our faith tradition who insist on there being an insurance policy for the faithful. The life of Job, Jesus the Son of God and the apostle Paul not to mention the catalogue in Hebrews 11 of those who endured the most horrific deaths including being sawn in two for their faith, bring such a demand into question. Mostly, this is predicated on a wrong reading of 1 Corinthians 10.13 which talks of temptation and not hard times.

Disability in a Cross-cultural Context

A network of studies on beliefs and attitudes on disability, in different cultural settings, was set up by Ingstad and Reynolds Whyte in 1995. This was one of the first collections of anthropological studies that focused on the social perception of disability.

Later, in recognition of the fact that disability is a culture-bound concept, an international study was conducted by Bedirhan et al. to assess the cross-cultural applicability of linguistic terms in current use for disability classification and assessment purposes.

Western View

Looking at different cultures in juxtaposition is a well-established method in anthropology for gaining perspective of one's own location.

Contrastive analysis makes it clear that underlying the western discourse on disability is an assumption that equality is the desired goal and this, problematically, is construed as synonymous with sameness or similarity. As stated earlier the etymology of the word 'handicap' reveals how this came to be the case. It originally referred to a game in which the winner paid a forfeit and the umpire held the money in his cap. The term later was used in regard to competition in which weaker partners were weighted to make them more equal players. Thus the term in imbued with notions of competition and attempts towards equality.

Dumont (1980) and Striker (1982) both draw attention to a worrying prospect for this emphasis on equality, namely, an intolerance of innate diversity and individualism leading to the denial of the social nature of persons. Striker states that the love of difference leads to a humane social life whereas the pursuit of similarity leads to rejection and repression. Striker has some important insights on the western construction of disability. He observes that it is the context of a centralist state that conceptualizes infirmity as a category that it never previously was and accords it definition, criteria and degrees of severity. He notes the paradox that people with impairments become a marked group with a social identity the purpose of which is to render them invisible and unmentionable (1982, p. 149).

Robert Murphy, in his analysis of North American society notes that disability is regarded as invisible and unspeakable as evidenced in the fact that children are raised not to point or comment on people's impairments in their presence. He sees a paradox in that nobody is meant to 'see' the one person whose presence is dominating everyone's consciousness. This again is because differences are meant to be compensated for in order for the goal of equality (conceived as similarity) to be maintained. Linked to this intolerance of difference is the concept of stigma noted by Goffman. We will see that the presence of difference is not universally conceived of as being problematic for example, Aud Talle, in researching the Maasai of Kenya notes that unlike in the western context the notion is *not* heavily charged with implications of social inferiority.

Differences Across Cultures

The many differences found in the literature can be divided into four sets. First, we will look at 'disability, attitudes and beliefs,' second, 'disability and stigma', third, 'disability and gender' and fourth 'disability and personhood'.

Disability, attitudes and beliefs

Bedirhan et al. note that issues raised by genetic causes of disability, and whether they are present at birth or not, are complex and viewed differently in societies where beliefs such as the doctrine of karma prevail (2001, p. 317). Robert Edgerton (1985) showed that attitudes towards people with mental impairments varied greatly across non-western cultures. Among the Punah Bah persons with mild mental impairment are considered half-human *stenga linou* and the impairment is said to be caused by the soul being no good. All forms of impairment range from negative discrimination to acceptance and right up to the positive attribution of supernatural powers, as seen with the Songye of Zaire who elevate some intellectually impaired children to the status of 'ceremonial', giving them special ceremonies believing them to have healing powers.

The Maasai of Kenya believe that disability is the result of social and cosmic disorder yet have strong moral codes dictating that a child is to be treated well whatever its condition and that all children should be treated with equal regard.

The scene across India was found to be diverse (the authors do not specify religion in their report which could also account for some of the diversity found). Bangalore demonstrated most support for disabled people, in contrast to Chennai where there was widespread stigma especially associated with mental impairment. A study of randomly selected villagers in Vellore in southern India, which examined attitudes towards individuals with physical impairments, revealed that 82 per cent of these attitudes were positive. Historically India has taken a positive attitude to persons with impairments and there are records of centres offering special care. In the entire country, only 20,000 persons with mental impairments are in specialized institutions. The rest are living in the community with their families. On the negative side societies made adverse assessments of the reason for disability, as:

- Ancestral displeasure (the Punah Bah of Sarawak believe that every new birth is the rebirth of an ancestor and an impaired baby is an expression of displeasure).
- Evidence of sexual sin (the Songye of Zaire and Punah Bah believe that the breaking of sex taboos, for example couples having sexual intercourse during the woman's pregnancy may lead to impairment. The Punah Bah also see twins as evidence of the breaking of this taboo and evidence of an insatiable sexual appetite).
- Generational sin (Nigeria; Maasai of Kenya (Ingstad and Reynolds Whyte 1995); also Greece, India and Japan (Bedirihan et al. 2001).
- Individual wrong doing and bad karma (Cambodia, Romania, Japan (Ingstad and Reynolds Whyte 1995).
- The result of sorcery (the preferred explanation of the Songye) (1998, p. 99).

On the positive side, some cultures demonstrate full acceptance of the disabled person as a full person and others see the person as a divine gift. This latter point should be seen critically and is probably not unconnected to the prevalence of negative explanations for disability. Ingstad notes from her research in Botswana:

> Another way to avoid the stigmatizing label is to claim that the child is mpho ya modimo 'a gift from God'. In line with Tswana tradition of giving children a name that is meaningful for the life situation of a child born into, or for the parents' wishes or expectations, several of the children in my sample born with visible impairments had been given this name. The Tswana traditional God Modimo, and even the Christian counterpart that has taken over the same name,

is mainly seen as a distant omnipotent power that demonstrates trust in people by giving them such special challenges. (1995, p. 254)

We will look finally at the belief that a disabled person is to be valued like any other human being. For the Songye of Zaire this positive view is a consequence of a more flexible and accepting attitude towards the vagaries of life in general. Devlieger remarks,

> a continuous effort of improving and accommodating the living conditions of persons with disabilities is basically a Western idea that is foreign to Songye thought. Instead the Songye have developed in their culture alternative ways and means of coping with disability. Living within the limits of the disability rather than surpassing them seems to be the most important norm. (1995, p. 95)

We should note here, perhaps a freedom from the 'superman/ superwoman' myth so popular in western values. Among the Punah Bah of Sarawak disability is not unspeakable as it is in western society and people speak freely in the presence of those with impairments and the impaired concerning their own. People are not singled out by nicknames connoting their impairment, largely because they have a soul and are recognized as full persons (Nicolaisen 1995, p. 48). However, Aud Talle notes that among the Maasai the naming of bodily characteristics does not have derogatory undertones; rather, such practices reveal a cultural acceptance of difference.

Disability and stigma

From our own cultural location it is easy to assume that disability entails stigma in all settings. Even within the UK stigma is attached to mental illness far more than other forms and this is seen to have been enhanced by media attention since Care in the Community became policy and an unjustified assumption that violence against the public and mental illness are linked. In fact, the causal links are the opposite way around: people with mental illnesses are more likely to be victims of attack rather than perpetrators. In Japan and Romania all forms of impairment lead to stigma. Bedirhan et al. argue: 'it is a consistent finding that people [in Japan] would say something negative about a person appearing in public who is obese, or intellectually slow' (2001, p. 154). In contrast it is found that the Dutch have a high level of tolerance for people with impairments who appear in public with the exception of those who manifest 'disturbing behaviour'. In India there is a high tolerance of 'deviant' behaviour and relatively low stigma unless, as in the Netherlands, the person's behaviour is disturbing. In Turkey people with physical or cognitive impairments are reported to encounter less stigma than persons with alcohol and drug-related problems.

Disability and gender

Gender, like disability, and indeed, a host of other things, is a social construct. Let us begin with an exotic example from the Punah Bah of Central Borneo who believe that men and women have more than one soul; one has six and the other seven and it is not difficult to guess which is one down! As is customary in patriarchal contexts, it is the woman who is deemed to be deficient.

Among the Maasai it seems that when blame is being apportioned it is not uncommon for the woman to be singled out as the guilty party. The ill health of one child was assumed to be the result of the mother's misconduct (Ingstad and Reynolds Whyte 1995, p. 65). At least in this case the mother had admitted some misconduct rather than the evidence of the sick child being regarded as concrete proof. Elsewhere the relations between co-wives is regarded as fertile ground for seeking the cause of disability. Talle notes that beliefs can be very forceful and especially when they concern the morals of women.

Robert Murphy (1995), an American anthropologist who

is a wheelchair user notes that he developed some very good relationships with women after the onset of his illness and he elects not to put this down to a stereotypical mothering instinct in women but rather to the removal of sexual threat (which he believes is always present in women in the presence of men). He insists, 'it forecloses an ancient power struggle and puts an end to 'male superiority'.

Whereas in western culture physical attractiveness is prized most highly for wives, in some African countries (for example Kenya, among the Maasai and in Botswana) hard work, efficient management and sociability are of primary importance and this would have implications for how disability is viewed.

Disability and personhood: egocentric and sociocentric concepts

As we shall see, features of disability vary hugely depending on a culture's concept of personhood. Tamasheq terms for a number of impairments include excessive freckles, protruding navel, absentmindedness and flabby or small buttocks. Most of these, unsurprisingly, are not on the WHO list as they do not fit with a biomedical view. The point to note is that these do not relate to classification but to the view of personhood as understood by the Tamasheq. In western society personhood is tied in with individual capability and accomplishment: among the Punah Bah of Central Borneo it is associated primarily with social relations as is the case in many societies based on kinship. In a good number of societies being a member of a family and having children are of greater importance than having the capacity to work or possessing good looks. The contrast between egocentric and sociocentric concepts of personhood provides a useful comparative framework. Among the Punah Bah of Sarawak, 'personhood is essentially the fulfilment of a socially significant career, of which parenthood is the alpha and omega' (Ingstad and Reynolds Whyte 1995, p. 50).

The Barbadian concept of personhood emphasizes a balance between autonomy and connectedness. Goerdt notes:

> At the same time that one should demonstrate autonomy, one must not be too independent of others ... for the unity of the group depends not only on the contribution of each member, but also on each member's willingness to accept help from others. (1984, p. 88)

Finally, it should be noted that attitudes are best when a society recognizes something of intrinsic worth in any given individual regardless of their condition. The Punah Bah believe that all offspring are reincarnations of ancestors and therefore must be respected because they see 'someone else' inside that body. This is of similar benefit to a Christian view that sees in each person the image of the Triune God. In this case too the person is to be well-treated because of that status.

Having established that attitudes to disability vary across cultures and yet it is not uncommon for people to assume its existence denotes a human failing, we now seek to establish the ubiquity of suffering in the human condition and explore the topic theologically. This is not to imply that disability intrinsically entails suffering, although socially it is likely to.

Suffering and the Contemporary World

In the western contemporary world the situation has been enflamed by the new atheists who take suffering in the world to be grounds for atheism. Suffering to some extent has always been part and parcel of life. This was accepted in earlier times, when people lived closer to the creation and appreciated the risks and vulnerability of the conditions for human life. Also the extended family and greater community living helped to offset the burden of much suffering. In our individualistic world with the nuclear family to the fore and medical science seeking to extend the lives of people almost indefinitely, without reference to quality of life for the person concerned, individuals are easily overburdened and crushed by the task in hand. Pressures associated with the advent of the nuclear family; the geographical break-up of families through social mobility in the wake of industrialization; the anonymity of life in the metropolis as compared to the close familiarity of the village scene; and the unchecked advance of medical science; all factors contributing to human suffering, must be laid at the door of humanity: not divinity.

Journalist Philip Yancey in *What Use is God* (2010) goes into geographical areas where disaster has struck and interviews the people on the ground to see how they feel. Interestingly he finds that while the global media broadcast the incident to people in their pleasant living rooms all over the world, where many, including the new atheists, shake their fists, the victims call out to God for help and relate the most heartening tales of rescue and deliverance. Not as if it had not happened, but they themselves are not full of the anger and rage that many detached onlookers often are. The Enlightenment has given us an unrealistic expectation that life will be easy now and so we demand the abolition of all discomforts. Older people (and probably more so women) are now engaged in a battle against the advance of any sign of old age. The eastern world in contrast values the advance of age with the benefits of greater wisdom and experience of life. We seem to be engaged in a war with our creator for the creation God has made. It is as if we have a dog and keep complaining at ways in which it fails to live up to the expectations we may have for a horse. The prophet Isaiah rebukes those who are made for arguing with the creator about his creation: 'You turn things upside down, as if the potter were thought to be like the clay' (Isa. 29.16). The heart of this must be seen as egocentricity.

Suffering, evil and the Disability Movement

It must be acknowledged that the issue of suffering is a thorny topic with the Disability Movement as some resent disability being glossed by outsiders as a form of suffering. The movement does not speak with one voice and some people with disabilities have ambivalent feelings; it has also been noted as being divided over the issue of impairment.

However, I have some sympathy with the dilemma and reflecting on some of my own tussles with gender I think I can understand the emotional charge, while seeing the root problem as being elsewhere. It would seem not to be so much a question of 'impairment' as what it argues for regarding inclusive practices. So I am hoping to take the heat out of including a section on suffering in this book on disability by pointing out that the issues that cause offence do not need to be part and parcel of the argument. Where our purpose is to include and qualify for participation we may be able to look at some unpopular matters without causing alienation.

Folkloric interpretations for the existence of disability and suffering in general abound, as we have seen. It is necessary to comment on the common conflation of evil and suffering. While evil invariably involves suffering, suffering may occur (even to an extreme degree) without any intimation of evil. The best and most commonplace illustration of this latter fact must surely be in the reality of childbirth. Women may suffer even to the point of death, yet childbirth is generally seen as a very positive event.

Hauerwas defines suffering in *Suffering Presence* as 'a brute power that does violence to our best laid plans' (1986, p. 165). Jesuit priest Paul Crowley offers a not dissimilar definition in *Unwanted Wisdom*: 'suffering is first and foremost the involuntary loss of an intrinsic good' (2005, p. 32). Clearly this would not ordinarily encompass the experience of childbirth, but where suffering more often crosses with evil and destructive forces then this is a useful definition.

Certainly in life there are experiences that come 'as a brute force' and 'do violence to our best laid plans' and disability is only one among many. As disabled feminist philosopher, Susan Wendell says, 'Every life has burdens, some of them far worse than disability' (1996, p. 154). In any difficult circumstance, bereavement, redundancy, natural disaster, etc., we are forced to grapple with how the world is and who God is in new ways and it could be argued that the worst of the suffering may be the violence it does to our best laid theology too! McGrath expresses this impact: 'Suffering possesses a double cutting edge: the sheer pain and distress of the experience is driven by an unbearable intensity by what that suffering might imply' (2000, p. 76). Frances Young speaks of this double impact when she says that Arthur (her intellectually impaired son) was not the main problem but the sense of abandonment by God that she felt. She also notes the link between doubt and an underlying emotional distress (Young 1990, p. 54).

We will examine now the attempt that philosophy makes to resolve the issue of an Almighty God with the existence of tribulation in the world. First we will look at the Enlightenment conundrum of theodicy which will be seen to be a futile debate.

The Enlightenment conundrum created by philosophy and classical theism: theodicy

The word 'theodicy' is a composite of two Greek stems: theos, meaning God and dike, meaning justice or righteousness. The term was coined by Leibniz as the title of his 1710 text which 'explains' how this world is the best of all possible worlds. In modern theodicy God, not humanity, is on trial and this is because of the problem that is foregrounded. Disablist theologian Tom Reynolds sums up the problem: 'the issue amounts to whether and how we can justify God's abiding love and sovereign purpose given the constancy and ubiquity of human suffering and brokenness' (2008, p. 29).

In recent times two camps have emerged: one that foregrounds the problem of pain and the other the issue of God's justice. The twentieth century intensified the historic problem as massive disasters such as Hiroshima, the Holocaust and other genocides were brought to our attention as well as natural disasters on a grand scale.

Summarizing the theodicy of Austin Farrer, Henderson and Hein caution against 'the prideful boasts of the homespun theologian'. An Enlightenment tendency is to reduce the shady and mixed to the clear and transparent at the price of idealizing the reality of evils. It tends to divide suffering neatly into human sin and natural suffering thus failing to name structural sins as evil.

Practical theodicy is a praxis-orientated approach which seeks more to promote a view of God as not detached from suffering, than to hold out abstract answers.

Finally, from a disability perspective, Reynolds who sees that theodicy is the pivotal issue concerning the awkward relationship between disability and theology, warns,

> theodicy questions, inevitable as they may be, can produce unintended but palpable mechanisms of exclusion that obviate the call to hospitality at the centre of Christian faith. Under the banner of love, the allegedly benign intention to understand, accept, help and heal disabilities can ironically stymie the genuine welcome of disabled persons into our communities, signifying a deeper and perhaps more pernicious exclusion. Hence we must proceed with great caution and circumspection in the attempt to discern God's hand in human disability. (2008, p. 30)

Philosophers David Hume and John Stuart Mill both show it is not possible to arrive at the all-powerful and wholly good God of Christian theism. (We can see here that what they call Christian Theism is in fact a classical overlay on the Christian God and as such is deism and a far cry from Trinitarian incarnational Christianity.) There is a view that since the concept of a loving God cannot be extrapolated from the data it must be a divine revelation, and certainly C. S. Lewis, while an atheist, was perplexed at where the notion of a loving God could have come from. We should perhaps remember that Lewis lost his mother at the age of nine and shortly afterwards was sent away to boarding school with his brother. They had a hard time there and the headteacher was certified as insane when the school closed down.

Finally, others retreat into divine mystery insisting that God's ways are not our ways. However, this oft quoted sentiment from the book of Isaiah contextually is about forgiveness (Isa. 55), thus demonstrating that God's ways are manifestly higher than our ways and not lower as would be the case in a context of gratuitous suffering. Forster takes issue with the argument that God is beyond reason stating that the Logos (a name for God) comes from the same root as our word 'logical' and therefore this attempt to dismiss the problem is bogus (2006).

While we stay within the classical framework we can make very little progress on this topic. Wendy Farley, departing from classical theology, offers a revisionist reading of God which succeeds in making God loving and co-suffering without being impotent.

She states that tragic vision is theistic and repudiates the metaphors of a savage or malevolent cosmos. It is not gnostic but shares with classical Christian theology a belief that creation is good. Farley insists on placing suffering rather than sin at the centre, not out of a desire to minimize sin but because she believes that suffering is a more important anomaly for Christian faith.

We now move towards a Trinitarian view of God, dispensing with Aristotle's Unmoved Mover, and embrace an incarnational God who suffers with us, in order to see the world differently and encounter a much more complex universe.

Trinitarian Theism and Incarnational Christianity

Within this framework we have to reconsider two main issues: namely, God's omnipotence and the reality of suffering in God's world. In this section God's sovereignty and omnipotence and the related question of might and power will be explored. The complexity of the universe and the Creator who made it will be underscored together with a theology of connection which can unexpectedly give rise to suffering. God's purpose of drawing us deeper into a relationship of love and freedom is then expounded.

Open theism

Some open theists like Roger Forster, take a limited view of the 'openness' of God, and while agreeing that God does not move every pawn on the board as this would violate the free will at work in the universe, nevertheless, takes the view that God being like a Master Chess player can still determine the final outcome without restricting the free decisions of other key players (Forster 2002, p. 6). Forster's view enables us to hold to the 'sovereignty of God' (but not the popular view that is naked fatalism) within a complex framework of the universe. God's own answer to Job involves an insistence on the complexity of human existence and cosmology (Job 38). We will unpack further the misconceptions that arise from a classical overlay regarding the sovereignty of God.

God's sovereignty

Much of our thinking on God's sovereignty is conditioned by Calvinism which sees absolutely everything that happens in history as being expressly God's will. Some illumination on this issue is brought by Costas Karras in his appraisal of the doctrine of the Trinity in relation to political thought and action. The matter hinges on our understanding of God's power:

> Once the distinction between the human way of comprehending power and God's way of exercising power is understood, we can be freed of the delusion that the broad currents of history must be God's work. Certainly God may and does act in history, but on the one hand his action is subject to no necessity while on the other he has granted autonomy to his creation of which man is the crown. Certainly there must have been currents of history pleasing to him, but to assume that whatever occurs is his will suggests either fatalism or else the choice of a comfortable but self-serving idolatry of our age (1991, p. 170).

Vardy positively rails against this kind of false conclusion laying bare its negative implications which those in anguish will readily detect.

> To hold that God plans each thread of our lives with care makes him into an obscene God, not a loving God. God does not want suffering, he does not will evil, he does not use suffering as a means to some wider end. Jesus fought against evils, he cried when Lazarus died. Compassion and God's tender care was central to his message. (1992, p. 119)

Roger Forster points to some consequences of this type of thinking which every evangelist and pastor should surely heed. He claims that Christianity went into decline in this country after two horrific world wars in which young men returned home deeply traumatized by what they had witnessed and, no doubt, participated in, only to be informed that this was the will of God (Forster 2006, p. 9). Thomas Oord explores the nature of God in his open and relational account of providence, *The Uncontrolling Love of God* (2015). Michael Howard in *God in the depths* (1999) challenges an assumption that in times of crisis the God of the Bible is about bringing superficial control rather than working deeply to bring about spiritual transformation. Christian psychologist Gerald May also posits that our demand for God to be in control is more an emotional and psychological attachment issue than a theological proposition (1991, pp. 111–12), and while I appreciate that this is a highly contentious issue I do now have some sympathy with this view. I would refer the interested reader to the work of Michael Lloyd in *Café Theology*, where in Chapter 3 he makes a thorough exploration of the issues that relate to God's Providence.

We also need to consider what the Christian God's power looks like. William Placher (1994) taking a Christological view argues that God's power is shown in weakness and vulnerability. Jesus on the cross embodies this truth as many onlookers taunted him assuming that if he was powerful he would come down from the cross: 'You are going to destroy the temple and build it in three days, save yourself! Come down' (Matt. 27.40). We might say that his power was best expressed in sacrificial love, unconditional forgiveness, and by fully entering into the human predicament.

Vardy states: 'to claim to understand the ways of God would be presumptive folly' (1992, p. 90). It is precisely this 'presumptive folly' that motivates Job's comforters and even some in the church today.

Paul Crowley wrote *Unwanted Wisdom* after the traumatic loss of two of his siblings. He reveals the unwelcome truth that wisdom and insight can come from an acutely engaged, insider position. He cautions against an over-individualistic interpretation of suffering for he sees that we live in a connected world. He simply puts it, 'very little that happens to us is so private, so much my own problem, that it does not have ripple effects (2005, p. 38). Moreover, Crowley cautions that suffering is irreducibly personal as it is people who suffer and not just populations, classes and groups (p. 27). Gutièrrez says: 'Job's words are a criticism of every theology that lacks compassion and contact with reality' (2005, p. 30). Disabled professor Stewart Govig complains that some preachers believe that 'tough times don't last, but that tough people do' (1989, p. 13). He insists: 'tough times last. To pretend otherwise is a romantic falsifying of truth. It only intensifies the non-sense of disease and disability. Yet healing and hope are also realities.'

In incarnational theology we are confronted by the centrality of the cross and therefore of suffering. The cross also instructs us of the fact that the power of the Christian God resides in weakness and not a show of might, as we see when Jesus was urged to come down off the cross! In Trinitarian theology we are reminded of the connectedness of all things. An over-individualistic worldview can assume that every small thing that happens is for our own personal good but if we take a connected stance then there must be times when what happens to us is simply part of a domino effect.

Wendy Farley in her groundbreaking *Tragic Vision and Divine Compassion* posits what she calls a contemporary theodicy which in my view avoids these pitfalls. For Farley, tragic vision locates the possibility of suffering in the conditions of existence and in the fragility of human freedom.

> The very structures that make human existence possible make us subject to the destructive power of suffering. Since guilt is not the primary problem, atonement and forgiveness cannot help transcend tragedy. Tragic suffering cannot be atoned for; it must be defied. Compassion is that power which survives to resist tragic suffering. (1990, p. 29)

Christian psychologist Gerald May in the Introduction to *The Dark Night of the Soul* brings this professional judgement which seems in concert with Farley's perceptions.

> But John of the Cross's insights have helped me understand that suffering does not result from some divine purgation designed for a spiritual elite. Instead, suffering arises from the simple circumstances of life itself. Sometimes human suffering is dramatic and horrifying. More often it is ordinary, humble, and quiet. But neither way is it 'God's will'. The divine presence doesn't intend us to suffer, but is instead *with* us in all the experiences of life, in both suffering and joy. And that presence is always inviting us towards greater freedom and love. (2004, p. 9)

Finally, Roger Forster (2006) and Keith Ward (1982), the latter being a former atheist, affirm that the purpose of human life is to be in a love relationship with God and others: the highest good in view is not pleasure but a love relationship with the Creator (Ward 1982). Added to this John of the Cross and Teresa of Avila insist that God is always calling us into new realms of freedom. That is perhaps the best lens through which to view all that happens in this world. One might question just how suffering is going to enhance this love relationship, although, strangely, that may be the case. In this vein, Farrer offers us this insight:

> God does not give us explanations; we do not comprehend the world, and we are not going to. It is, and it remains for

us, a confused mystery of bright and dark. God does not give us explanations; he gives us a Son ... A Son is better than an explanation. (1960, p. 27)

The quest for answers is fuelled by the intensity of inner pain and yet answers do not relieve the pain overmuch but an encounter with the Son certainly can. In point of fact, this is circular as arguments do not relieve the pain in the heart yet it requires some progress there in order for those in pain to feel encouraged to move towards the Son.

Jesuit, Paul Crowley, who is influenced by Rahner, talks about 'a theological reflection that takes seriously the concreteness of the human experience of suffering as a place where the holiness of God can be encountered' (Crowley 2005, p. 19).

The Centrality of the Cross and the Suffering of God

Having moved away from classical Theism into incarnational Christianity we must be mindful that the cross is the central motif that alone makes sense of God's loving involvement with his creation. We will begin by exploring the issue of Holy Saturday and then by discussing the suffering of God, followed by a consideration of the question of redemptive suffering and the indications that suffering can produce some creative outcomes.

Alan Lewis in *Between Cross and Resurrection* (2001) explores the meaning of Holy Saturday in the Easter narrative. It is necessary here to offer a definition of the concept of Holy Saturday. It is the second day of the Easter drama and, as such, is characterized by a sense of total desolation and godforsakenness as Jesus lies dead in the tomb. It is a day of deep darkness where everything is defeat. Admittedly it is the eve of Easter Sunday but that is not known from the vantage point of Saturday, therefore it is a day of deep gloom and hopelessness. Alan Lewis, a promising young theologian, wrote this book while dying from cancer, so once again we have a sharp insider perspective.

Importantly, Lewis concludes that a Holy Saturday identity

defines not what it is to be a Christian but what it is to be human. Perhaps in this issue of suffering and evil we need to self-identify first as human and only after as Christian, for the answer to our plight lies more in regard to the universal human condition from which we as believers are not exempt. Moreover, to identify as Christians at all is to worsen the problem as the New Testament makes clear – for we are in a battle. The life of Paul is a startling example as there can be no doubt that much of the pain that he experienced could have been avoided had he not become a follower of Jesus with missionary zeal.

To those who suffer without knowing why, it is helpful to understand the degree to which Jesus suffered. Alan Lewis, who must have been confronted with the loss of his assumed bright future says: 'How can we do otherwise than speak to our suffering world of a suffering God?' (2001, p. 164). Lewis is concerned that we have a habit of rushing on to the end of the Easter story in order to make it all right. Human beings have a tendency to want to push life stories into a schema of 'they all lived happily ever after'. However, Lewis is clear that the joy of Easter Sunday does not remove the desolation of Holy Saturday. And so it is with us. We have to face our Holy Saturdays head-on in all their starkness, with the hope of Easter Sunday ahead of us which gives us hope but does not diminish the pain. Alan Lewis writes: 'and the confusion of emotion lies ... in the additional bitterness of knowing that the final scene of joy cannot be reached without the enduring of heartbreak first' (2001, p. 77).

Images of the holy easily become sacrosanct images. Our idea of God is not a divine idea. It has to be shattered time after time. C. S. Lewis insists:

> He shatters it himself ... Could we not almost say that this shattering is one of the marks of his presence? The incarnation is the supreme example; it leaves all previous ideas of the Messiah in ruins. And most are 'offended' by the iconoclasm; and blessed are those who are not. (1961, pp. 55–6)

As implied in the quotation above there are images of God that we are more drawn to but which may get shattered, and so we are continually in the business of allowing God to remake our image of the divine. This is no comfortable affair and nowhere less so than when we turn to the issue of to what degree God himself suffers.

The idea that God suffers with his creation has become prominent in modern Christian thought, challenging the Medieval and patristic concept of an impassable God. Fiddes (1988) identifies four reasons for this. The first is found in a psychological view of the nature of love which is seen as participative and sympathetic. The second is drawn from a Christological view and a theology of the cross. The third is part of the defence against God for creating this world as he must share in the consequences of the risks accrued from freedom. Finally, as stressed by process theology, the world is seen as a living organism and thus God too must grow and suffer with his world. Fiddes, who lost his son, argues that the participation of God in suffering as in the atonement, has a transforming effect upon human personalities:

> The psychological effect upon a sufferer of being aware of a suffering God who understands his [sic] predicament may be below the level of theological argument, but it may in the end soar on wings far higher than any formal theodicy can. (1988, p. 31)

On the psychological level, it could also be argued that it panders to our baser need for revenge too. This can, perhaps, be seen in C. S. Lewis's outburst: 'Sometimes it is hard not to say: "God forgive God". Sometimes it is hard not to say so much. But if our faith is true, He didn't. He crucified Him' (Lewis 1961, p. 25).

It must be noted that feminist theology is ambivalent on a suffering God. Brown and Parker object that:

> the suffering God theologies continue in a new form the traditional piety that sanctions suffering as imitation of the

holy one. Because God suffers and God is good, we are good if we suffer. If we are not suffering we are not good. To be like God is to take on the pain of all. (1989, p. 19)

However, the notion of a co-suffering God continues to be particularly significant to womanist, mujerista and minjung theologians (Slee 2003, p. 68). On a more positive note Frances Young insists that the suffering of God is not just a theological theory but a devotional necessity (2007, p. 237).

However, it must be accepted that in as much as God knows and understands our pain because of what he suffered on the cross, it is a source of comfort without us having to take pleasure in the suffering of God. Human beings need to feel understood and the fact that only God can understand when others cannot is surely of value. Perhaps this is why we say irritating and fatuous things like: 'I know exactly how you feel', when it is clear that we do not and cannot. Whatever psychological and emotional value there may be, we must take a theological look at this question and we shall see that the debate centres around just how far we think we should push the suffering of God.

Thus, some of our homespun theologies of suffering arise from our demand for life to be straightforward and readily comprehensible. However, as we have seen, life as God has made it is far from being easily accessible to our human minds. While it is true that we need to become as children – in our capacity to trust – there is nothing childish or uncomplicated about the message of the cross for at its heart there resides a total contradiction, or paradox, perhaps? In addition there is a need to balance the reality of suffering with some of the more positive expectations of the Christian life.

Redemptive Suffering?

Finally, we come to the contentious question, which the context of the cross also raises: to what extent, if at all, is suffering redemptive? Henderson and Hein (2001, p. 109) quote Farrer as saying: 'The event of the cross clearly indicates that God takes suffering to be the pathway to redemption.'

Certainly it tells us that the suffering of *Jesus* is central to *our* redemption, but to what degree we can extrapolate from that that *our* suffering is redemptive is highly questionable. It might be objected that if all suffering is purely and simply redemptive why did Jesus spend so much of his ministry interfering with this therapeutic effect of suffering? John says that Jesus came 'to destroy the devil's work' (1 John 3.8) and that brief seems to have led him to remove a lot of earthly sorrow and pain.

A further objection to the view that suffering is redemptive is articulated in liberation theology which takes issue with this view for the effect that it has upon the project of social justice and the fight to remove all sources of oppression. If suffering is for our redemption, then we would hesitate to offer relief to anyone in difficulty. However, Alister McGrath expresses the reverse view, stating: 'By working to lessen the suffering of God's world and God's people, we are easing his heartache over their pain' (2000, p. 103).

While there are diverse views about suffering one wonders if the debate would benefit from a definition of suffering, for some views are so relentlessly upbeat that it is tempting to think that suffering could be defined in lesser terms than those who take a more sober view. However, I suspect that the spectrum is so widely ranged because some have an eye on the experience of suffering while others are likely to have more an eye to God's nature and purposes. For example, this quote by Kathryn Tanner could well be embracing a Thomist position predicated on the unfailing goodness of God when she asserts:

The world is perfected by being brought into closer relations with the God who perfects it. In union with God, in being brought near to God, all the trials and sorrows of life – suffering, loss, moral failing, the oppressive stunting of opportunities and vitality, grief, worry, tribulation and strife – are purified, remedied and reworked through the gifts of God's grace. (2001, p. 2)

Crowley grounds his writing in his own desperate experience and makes use of a graphic quotation from Karl Rahner about the suffering of bereavement: 'and thus, as death has trodden roughly through my life, every one of the departed has taken a piece of my heart with him and often enough my whole heart' (1960, p. 54). Towards the end of his career, Rahner gave a short address entitled 'Christian pessimism' in which he speaks of the 'radical perplexity' of human life. Taking 2 Corinthians 4.8 'We are ... perplexed but not in despair' as his text, Rahner claimed that perplexity was an integral part of human existence.

Rabbi Blumenthal in his exploration of the experiences of Holocaust victims and victims of child abuse also takes a less upbeat position than Tanner. Wendy Farley, who also seems to have an eye on the lived experiences of suffering humanity, sees 'certain kinds of suffering as irredeemably unjust' (1990, p. 22). However, there is a very helpful creative tension in Farley's paradigm, for while she is insistent that suffering is not redeemable and even all God's compassionate love poured out into the world cannot put right or undo all the horror that tragic vision has occasioned, neither is the hope of a pain-free future sufficient consolation; nevertheless she sees suffering as the soil from which divine compassion is harvested in our own lives for compassion as an enduring disposition presupposes knowledge of suffering (p. 75). Therefore there is a sense in which suffering is both the problem and must play a part in the 'solution'. Her vision of redemption is greater and more credible than merely attempting to make the horror of suffering redemptive. She writes:

> Tragedy presses upon us a dark vision of reality, but it is in turn transcended by the apprehension of ultimate goodness. Its appeal to justice and its evocation of compassion are traces of an ethical order that is frustrated but not destroyed by unjust suffering. (p. 29)

There is, however, a third position which is harder still to prove but which does face the horror of the lived experiences of some believers and manage to maintain a firm footing on a belief in both the goodness and the providence of Almighty God. This view is commonly known as 'the dark night of the soul' as explicated by the sixteenth-century Spanish Carmelite monk, St John of the Cross. His view (and that of Teresa of Avila, his mentor) is that there are times of great difficulty and suffering in the lives of believers but that during those dark times God is doing some deep but hidden work that will bring the believer to greater union with his or her Lord. It does not minimize the distress of suffering but rather is predicated on an uncannily profound understanding of the complexity of human beings (four centuries before Freud). It argues that the dark night is designed to bypass our defence mechanisms and dismantle things while we are unaware as otherwise we would obstruct this work – all of this bringing us to greater freedom from attachments and compulsions. Crowley testifies that there are times when the suffering that accompanies tragic reversal, forces upon us a wisdom that is not sought nor even desired yet, wonderfully, this same wisdom can become the key to a joyous freedom 'where one discovers, all of a sudden, as if awakened from a long trance, that what once seemed very important simply no longer has any power over us' (2005, p. 147).

Vardy says that 'God does not *use* suffering ...' (my emphasis). There is a certain ambiguity here. In context he may be saying that God does not choose suffering as a tool in the sense that God would be the agent behind the suffering. However, there is another possible view which considers that while God does not intend suffering for us that where suffering occurs God most certainly aims to use it for our own good and that of others. Many popular Christian writers express the view that God uses affliction to form us and perfect us (Derek Prince, C. S. Lewis, Selwyn Hughes, Alister McGrath and Edith Schaeffer), although it may not always be clear if they think that means God intends it or allows it and transforms it. Certainly Prince believes that it is intentional as in *Chords from David's Harp*, he speaks of God knowing exactly how high to heat the furnace of affliction to cause the dross to come to the surface

(1983, p. 109). Theologian Mary Grey objects to this popular notion of what she calls 'God the pedagogue'.

This assumption of God behind all affliction may simply be as theologian Frances Young (2014) reveals:

> God in the Judeao-Christian tradition has always been the originator of all things and the ultimate victor, even if there be a devil upsetting his worlds for the time being. (p. 30) Even when Satan appears he is often depicted as God's policeman or training officer, the one who sets tests of character, who brings accusations in the heavenly court, rather than being God's hostile opponent (the book of Job for example) The fundamental biblical view is that the only real ultimate is God. (p. 31)

Biggar (1998) and Bretherton (2006) argue that there is a weak and a strong type of redemptive suffering, a strong form being found in situations of unjust suffering where the believer is identified with Christ and submits to the Father's will. A weaker form would be, in not specifically making up the sufferings of Christ, but having value, nonetheless, and not being pointless or meaningless.

If we turn to the New Testament we see that God refused to remove Paul's affliction as he could use it. Paul is expected to become stronger as a result of his weakness (2 Cor. 12.9). Paul also, underlining our connectedness in the Body of Christ, teaches that we can use our sorrows in order to comfort others who go through the same pain (2 Cor. 1.4). While it must be objected that God is not the *author* of suffering as 'he has compassion on all he has made' (Psalm 145.9), there is biblical evidence (not to mention a host of anecdotal evidence too) that God does not waste our suffering and uses it productively *provided that we cooperate with him*. McGrath in *Why Does God Allow Suffering?* argues that because Jesus went to the cross and we are called to follow him that believers should not expect to avoid suffering in their lives and that it can lead to good (McGrath 2000, p. 9).

Edith Schaeffer in *Affliction* (1978), and elsewhere, gives another angle that is helpful, as it moves way beyond a desire to 'fix' things and yields to a trusting relationship with a loving Creator. She uses a number of different images to express the same concept and I will work with her image of the museum. She imagines that in heaven there is a museum with two large halls in it. Each believer's life is in the halls. In some parts of each life there was the overcoming victory model that was characterized by a change in circumstances and those are recorded in hall A. However, each one also has life experiences where circumstances did not change and the challenge to the believer was to 'overcome' in the teeth of the adverse circumstances. Her idea is based on the book of Job where we see a battle royal in the heavenly realm where Satan tempts Job to curse God because of all the adversity that has befallen him, and also on Hebrews 11 which gives a catalogue of those who overcame by the blood of the Lamb – the first set in positive events and the second in persevering despite such things as believers 'being sawn in two'! She urges us to see in our suffering an opportunity to honour God and not withdraw our love and trust as a powerful sacrifice of worship and as a lethal blow against Satan, God's enemy (1978, p. 76). This understanding can give us something constructive to offer a person in distress, in fact, she claims to have had this insight while comforting a dying friend who felt he could no longer do anything worthwhile. Nigel Biggar brings a similar insight about suffering even in the context of dying:

> A life is valuable not only for what it builds, but also for what it says. So in the faithful, hopeful, charitable manner of my suffering I may be able to demonstrate salvific truths about, for example, the contingent value of the human individual, the gracious goodness of God and the humanizing prospect of eternal life. (1998, p. 40)

Suffering threatens us as it confronts us with our utter powerlessness to control the world in which we live. Farley points this out in graphic detail leaving us no place to hide.

Once human suffering is possible, nothing restricts its range so that the kindest, or the weakest, or the most admirable people will be magically protected from it. Nothing limits suffering in its intensity, from driving people to despair through grief, pain or cruelty. Once suffering is posited as an essential component of human existence, radical suffering threatens every person. No one is protected from suffering that is so terrible that it breaks the spirit ... Suffering is a natural component of embodied, historical experience. (1990, p. 34)

However, there is a positive side here as it rightly aligns us with our creaturehood; for as human beings we are limited. We see that this experience of suffering indicates *not* necessarily that something has gone badly awry but conceivably that we are in the flow of God's purposes. McGrath states: 'The Christian Church is an extension of the passion of Christ. We are called to be members of the suffering people of God' (2000, p. 33).

McGrath argues that suffering produces maturity (p. 56), thus we could say the demand for the Christian life to be free of pain is an insistence on a superficial and immature faith. In addition, 'suffering often brings out the full potential in human beings, unleashing a creativity which is too easily stifled by smugness and security' (p. 56).

Amy Carmichael (Irish missionary to India for 55 years) is but one of many godly people in whose service for Christ much suffering was endured. Her poem, sometimes used as a hymn, brings a fresh perspective to this common fact among the saints.

No Scar

Hast thou no scar?
No hidden scar on foot, or side, or hand?
I hear thee sung as mighty in the land;
I hear them hail thy bright ascendant star.
Hast thou no scar?

Hast thou no wound?
Yet I was wounded by the archers; spent
Leaned me against a tree to die; and rent
By ravening beasts that compassed Me, I swooned.
Hast thou no wound?

No wound? No scar?
Yet, as the Master shall the servant be,
And pierced are the feet that follow Me.
But thine are whole; can he have followed far
Who hast no wound or scar?

Sometimes we are fellow sufferers simply on account of what life has dealt us, at other times we can be fellow sufferers by choice – not grimly pursuing suffering and pain but perhaps refusing to take the softer option for the sake of the gospel. 'They triumphed over him by the blood of the Lamb and by the word of their testimony; they did not love their lives so much as to shrink from death' (Rev. 12.11).

I would like to pay respect here to Sue and Andy Wheeler, former missionaries in Sudan, who I am privileged to know. In *Bombs, Ruins and Honey* Andy tells something of their story and the great struggle they had to interpret the suffering that encompassed them and the people around them in war-torn Sudan. Sue nearly died in Sudan, in the early years of their marriage. Andy writes:

> For Sue this was a crucial time in which her faith and her understanding of life was dismantled and a process of reconstruction began. We had both grown up in a Conservative non-conformist tradition which did not find it easy to cope with unrelenting suffering. Faith and prayer were the gateways to God's blessing and healing. These attitudes were often strengthened by the Charismatic renewal movement by which we, as well as other mission workers around us, had been influenced. Already on arriving in Sudan Sue found her faith challenged by the suffering around her to which there seemed no easy answer, or even any answer at all.

To have the first three years of our marriage consumed by unrelenting sickness and weakness did not square with the framework of faith with which Sue and I had grown up. (Wheeler 2006, p. 38)

However, later they took advice to return to England and the local women wept as they did not expect to ever see Sue again, knowing she was desperately ill. Once back in England, with Sue still far from well, they decided to return to Sudan. The people were deeply touched by this act of love and commitment to them, being more accustomed to expats packing up and fleeing in tough circumstances. They read this bold act to mean that the Wheelers felt a sense of belonging to them and the relationships moved on to a deeper level as a result.

We should not underestimate the impact of such an act on a people who probably felt bereft of God in their circumstances. Philip Yancey in *Where is God When it Hurts* says that there are times when it is as if God cannot reveal his love but in such times we may be vehicles of that love to one another in the Body of Christ. Perhaps the Wheelers' costly return put substance to the promise 'Never will I leave you; never will I forsake you' (Heb. 13.5) when everything else may have communicated the reverse. If we take a connected view of our humanity, as the Wheelers did, this act of solidarity may have been just what God could use. Interestingly Sue's church could only surmise that she had been sent to Sudan to meet her husband (2006, p. 38), not a priority of discipleship ever taught or indeed modelled by Jesus.

Added to this, Alan Lewis and Letty Russell both show that it is not always possible to know what is good and what is bad. Russell loses the sight in one eye and through it grows in courage: becoming at one and the same time both stronger and weaker (1993, p. 103). And there is the case of Mary Semple who believed that her facial deformities were used by God to free her from an abusive marriage.

As we begin to see that suffering is normative in the Christian life (indeed, the human life), then we are able to bring the only real comfort we can; namely, that of fellow sufferer which

Govig sees may be a 'better sign of hope' for the world than are the schemes of those who promise paradise' (1989, p. 115). Even Paul regarding his 'thorn in the flesh' came to a deeper understanding of its purpose in his life. Initially he regarded it as a messenger of Satan (which does not need to be disputed) but finally he came to recognize what has been termed 'the divine passive'– to acknowledge divine activity behind demonic initiatives. Albl states: 'He sees that the disability, even if instrumentally associated with the demonic, is ultimately of divine origin and has a divine purpose' (2007, p. 157).

Why Include This in This Book

Ambiguity is at the very heart of Christianity, as we worship a God who is fully human while being fully divine. Kierkegaard (alias Climacus) in *Philosophical Fragments,* contrasts two possible responses to the paradoxical claim that Jesus is both God and man. The two possible responses are faith or offence. These same two responses are what are before us in the paradoxical case of suffering and the purposes of a loving God. We can either keep our hearts open in a trusting attitude of faith or close our hearts in wounded offence. More stories relevant to this are explored in the next chapter where the concept of a disabled God is discussed.

It also demonstrates that the onus is on the church to facilitate people moving closer into love relationships (with God directly and with God through the Body of Christ) when in deep pain, rather than being further alienated through half-baked theologies of guilt and blame. The role of fellow-suffer is a productive one and one that can only have potency if, in Farley's terms, we have been able to garner divine compassion from our own sufferings. Also an incarnational view of God enables us to revalorize vulnerability and brokenness. The Christian view of suffering bestows more dignity than a patronizing response of 'poor you'. While it has been argued that suffering is not redemptive per se as we have seen, it can have redemptive potential.

I set out to do this work on inclusion of impaired believers not because I had any personal point of identification with 'disability' but because I had experienced exclusion based on embodiment (for being a woman) and was passionate for all people to be actively included and valued in the church. However, strangely, as I continued on my journey (far longer than expected due to the disruption of two major bereavements), I became immersed in this reality through the prolonged illness of my son who was unable to attend school (nor study at home) for several years during the vital GCSE years on account of CFS/ME. After the sudden and premature death of my brother, I immersed myself in literature on suffering as my former theological framework left me floundering and feeling deeply let down.

Our son became a shadow of his former self, becoming withdrawn and unable to socialize as before. He had been a fun-loving, happy and conscientious boy who was always on the go; full of ideas. I was shocked when one of the head teachers at his school with responsibility for children with special needs referred to my son's 'disability'.

Although the experience was heart-rending, I tried not to resent it as I realized that it meant I was entering the pain of many of the people I had wanted to support. I genuinely felt that the experience was incarnational and one day in church I was singing a song that goes 'be glorified in me, be glorified in me' and the words came into my head very forcefully: 'be crucified in me'. I did not change the words I was singing, but I had the realization that there was an element of Jesus being crucified in me in order to be glorified through this further suffering we were undergoing as a family.

Disabled, feminist, writer and researcher, Jackie Leach-Scully (2002), says that because disability is socially constructed it is not possible to know the irreducible core of suffering that exists with disability itself. Certainly, I experienced the pain of being in a world that only values certain outcomes and with the prospect that this bright boy (our only child and the only grandchild on both sides of the family) might not even get any GCSEs! A mother of a Downs' son told me in interview from

my original research that her son had had some physical problems and one time had to go into hospital for an operation.
She was afraid that he might die and was deeply hurt when her
own mother said that it might not be a bad thing if he didn't
pull through. Although shocking, it is perhaps not surprising
that a grandmother can feel like that – living as we do in a
society that devalues all who cannot make a contribution to
society. In our case we had the advantage that the prognosis
was good with the expectation of a full recovery, albeit a pain-
fully slow and erratic one. Only one mother was interviewed
in the original research, but her experience confirmed what I
had read in the literature about people with disabled children.

Points for Discussion and/or Reflection

1 What aspects of this chapter on suffering did you find
   most helpful or most unconvincing?
2 Do you think suffering is a core element in the Christian
   experience; both for the Messiah and all his disciples?
3 Do you think a theology of suffering is helpful when it
   comes to coping with the shock of some of life's struggles
   and trials?

References

Albl, M., 'For whenever I am weak then I am strong: Disability in Paul's
   epistles', in Avalos, H. (2007), *This Abled Body*, Atlanta: Society of
   Biblical literature.
Bedirhan, T., Chatterji, S., Rehm, J., Saxena, S., Bickerbach, J., Trotter,
   R., Room, R. (eds) (2001), *Disability and Culture: universalism and
   diversity*, Massachusetts: Hogrefe and Huber Publishers.
Biggar, N. (1998), 'God, the Responsible Individual and the Value of
   Human Life and Suffering', in *SCE* 11(1), p. 28–47.
Bretherton, L. (2006), *Hospitality as Holiness*, Aldershot: Ashgate.
Brown, J. C. and Parker, J. (1989) 'For God so loved the World? in J. C.
   Brown and C. R. Bohn (eds), *Christianity, patriarchy and abuse: a
   feminist critique*, pp. 139–60, New York: Pilgrim Press.

Climacus (1985) (alias Kierkegaard), *Philosophical Fragments*, Princeton: Princeton University Press.

Crowley, P. (2005), *Unwanted Wisdom: Suffering, the cross and hope*, New York: Continuum.

Devlieger, P. (1995), 'Why Disabled? The cultural understanding of physical disability on African society', in Ingstad and Whyte, *Disability and Culture*, Berkeley: University of California Press, pp. 94–106.

Dumont, L. (1980), *Homo Hierarchicus: The caste system and its implications*, Chicago: University of Chicago Press.

Edgerton, R. (1985), *The Cloak of Competence: stigma in the lives of the mentally retarded*, Princeton: University of California Press.

Farley, W. (1990), *Tragic Vision and Divine Compassion: a contemporary theodicy*, Louisville: John Knox Press.

Farrer, A. (1960), 'The Country Doctor.' In *Said or Sung*, World: London, pp. 34–47.

Fiddes, P. (1988), *The Creative Suffering of God*, Oxford: Clarendon Press.

Forster, R. (2002), *The Kingdom of Jesus*, Carlisle: Authentic Lifestyle.

Forster, R. (2006), *Suffering and the love of God: The book of Job*, London: Push Publishing.

Goerdt, A. (1984), *Physical Disability in Barbados: A cultural perspective*, Ann Arbor: University Microfilms.

Govig, S. (1989), *Strong at the broken places*, Louisville: John Knox Press.

Gutièrrez, G. (2005), *On Job: God talk and the suffering of the innocent*, New York: Orbis Books.

Hauerwas, S. (1986), *Suffering Presence*, Edinburgh: T & T Clark.

Henderson, E. and Hein, D. (2001), *Captured by the Crucified: The practical theology of Austin Farrer*, Edinburgh: T & T Clark.

Howard, M. (1999), *God in the depths*, London: SPCK.

Ingstad, B. and Reynolds Whyte, S. (1995), *Disability and Culture*, Berkeley: University of California Press.

Karras, C. (1991), *The Forgotten Trinity*, A. Heron (ed.), 3: 137–57, London: British Council of Churches.

Leach Scully, J. (2002), 'Drawing Lines, Crossing Lines: Ethics and the challenge of disabled embodiment', Paper given at the Britain and Ireland School of Feminist Theology 29 July.

Lewis C. S. (1961), *A Grief Observed*, London: Faber & Faber.

Lewis, A. (2001), *Between Cross and Resurrection*, Grand Rapids: Eerdmanns.

Lloyd, M. (2005), *Café Theology*, London: Alpha International.

May, G. (2004), *The Dark Night of the Soul*, San Francisco: Harper.

May, G. (1991), *Addiction and Grace*, New York: Harper One.

McGrath, A. (2000), *Why Does God Allow Suffering?* London: Hodder Christian Essentials.

Murphy, R. (1995), 'Encounters: the body silent in America', in Ingstad, B. and Reynolds Whyte, S., *Disability and Culture*, Berkeley: University of California Press, pp. 140–58.

Nicolaisen, I. (1995), 'Persons and Nonpersons: Disability and personhood among the Punah Bah of Central Borneo', in Ingstad, B. and Reynolds Whyte, S., *Disability and Culture*, Berkeley: University of California Press, pp. 38–55.

Oord, T. (2015), *The Uncontrolling Love of God*, Illinois: IVPAcademic.

Placher, W. (1994), *Narratives of a vulnerable God: Christ, theology and scripture*, Louisville Kentucky: Westminster John Knox Press.

Prince, D. (1983), *Chords from David's Harp*, Grand Rapids: Zondervan, Chosen Books.

Rahner, K. (1960), *Encounters with Silence*, trans. James Demske, Westminster: Newman Press.

Reynolds, T. (2008), *Vulnerable Communion*, Michegan: Brazos Press.

Russell, L. (1993), *Church in the Round*, Kentucky: Westminster/John Knox Press.

Schaeffer, E. (1978) *Affliction*, London: Solway.

Slee, N. (2003), *Faith and Feminism: An introduction to feminist theology*, London: Darton Longman & Todd.

Striker, H. J. (1982), *Corps infirmes et societies*, Paris: Aubier Montaigne.

Swinton, J., Mowat, H. and Baines, S. (2001), 'Whose Story am I? Redescribing Profound Intellectual Disability in the Kingdom of God', in *Journal of Religion, Disability and Health*, 15, pp. 5–19.

Talle, A. (1995), 'A child is a child: disability and equality among the Kenya Maasai', in Ingstad, B. and Reynolds Whyte, S., *Disability and Culture*, Berkeley: University of California Press, pp. 56–72.

Tanner, K. (2001), *Jesus, Humanity and the Trinity*, Edinburgh: T & T Clark.

Vardy, P. (1992), *The Puzzle of Evil*, London: Fount.

Ward, K. (1982), *Holding Fast to God: A reply to Don Cupitt*, London: SPCK.

Wendell, S. (1996), *The Rejected Body*, New York and London: Routledge.

Wheeler, A. (2006), *Bombs, Ruins and Honey*, Nairobi: Paulines Publications Africa.

Yancey, P. (2010), *What Use is God?* London: Zondervan.

Yancey, P. (1997), *Where is God When it Hurts*, Grand Rapids: Zondervan.

Young, F. (2014), *Arthur's Call*, London: SPCK.

Young, F. (1990), *Face to Face: A narrative essay in the theology of suffering*, Edinburgh: T & T Clark.

Young, F. (2007), *Brokenness and Blessing: Towards a Biblical Spirituality*, London: Darton, Longman & Todd.

Summary

This chapter has continued the debate on normality by extending the discussion to disability across many different cultures. It has been noted that folkloric notions of disability due to human misconduct abound in global contexts and also often obliquely in western societies. The research data of Bedirham et al. is set out under four disability headings: attitudes and beliefs; stigma; gender; and personhood: egocentric and sociocentric. On account of the negative causal relationship often assumed between family members and disability, the chapter has sought to overturn such thinking and further establish that suffering is inevitable in this life. An exploration of suffering was made, starting with the position of the new atheists who take the existence of suffering in the world as proof of atheism. From here the theology of suffering was unpacked in order to bring some clarity to a problem that is often raised in this context. Here we have noted a conundrum created by philosophy and classical theism, and under this heading we have considered the notion of theodicy. Classical theism is dispensed with in favour of Trinitarian theism and incarnational Christianity in order to establish that God suffers with us. The cross of Christ is seen to be the central motif here. The issue of redemptive suffering is explored and rejected in its usual form. The chapter closes with a personal account from the author and a rationale for inclusion of the subject in this work.

5

Fresh Theological Perspectives

In this chapter fresh theological perspectives on disability are explored. The issues of preaching and homiletics, hermeneutics and biblical interpretation are addressed. Also, matters concerning ecclesiology, liberation theology, and some key revisions of doctrine for disability, some of which are contentious. This chapter does include some complex words which can be found in the Glossary at the end of the book.

While it will be seen (in the next chapter) that there are some welcome initiatives with church for people with learning disabilities going on, there is also some useful theologizing taking place which engages critically with 'why we do church the way we do it' and seeks to challenge some of this rationale. The church is still a major influencing factor in society as it influences both individuals and communities so Arne Fritzon and Samuel Kabue (in *Interpreting Disability: A Church of All and for All*), both disability activists in the global church, caution that 'its appropriate understanding and interpretation of disability is crucial to how individual church members will relate to persons with disabilities, both spiritually and socially'. Avalos et al. (2007) in *This Abled Body: Rethinking Disabilities in Biblical Studies* explain that 'the realization that texts can mean the opposite of what we have thought them to mean lies at the very heart of our mission for this book'.

Linguistic Issues for Disability Inclusion: Hermeneutics, Homiletics and Metaphors

While there are some fresh expressions of church, as we shall see, there are also some fresh theological concepts that foreground disability and some interpretative keys, through an understanding of hermeneutics to mine wisdom from some of the disability narratives. There are some hard texts in all sacred Scriptures that require interpretation and pastoral sensitivity as a superficial interpretation may be oppressive and excluding.

A hermeneutic of suspicion

Weiss Block advises that interpretation of the Scriptures should start with a 'hermeneutic of suspicion' that seeks to uncover any bias in the narratives (in this case ableism) which could contribute to marginalization. Scottish minister and writer Graham Monteith in *Deconstructing Miracles: From thoughtless indifference to honouring disabled people* raises a number of issues around interpretation. He emphasizes, 'Christianity is an inclusive religion and inclusiveness without love is tokenism and is bound to lead to disappointment and patronization. To exclude is a sinful rejection of a major facet of the gospels' (Monteith 2005, p. 12). Monteith and Weiss Block (2002) are concerned that biblical interpretation should be wary of a 'quick fix' mentality. In place of this Monteith is encouraged by the recent trend to 'build on the foundation of Christian anthropology which emphasizes the giftedness of each (Pauline theology) and imago Dei' (2005, p. 65).

Normate hermeneutics

Wynn draws on the phrase 'normate hermeneutics' (a phrase coined by Rosemarie Garland-Thompson) to highlight what we find in biblical studies. If we understand hermeneutics as an interpretive lens with which we approach texts then normate identifies the cultural lens of 'normality' as Wynn explains, in traditional American culture the normate is an able-bodied white protestant male heterosexual. The further one moves from the normate image, the more powerless and margin-alized one becomes ... The 'normate hermeneutic' is the means by which scripture is interpreted so that it complies with and reinforces the socially contructed norms. (Wynn in Avalos et al. 2007, p. 92)

Preaching and homiletics

A minefield can exist where modern speakers seek to extrapo-late important insights from the healing narrative texts written in a dissimilar era when disability itself was construed very differently. Kathy Black's table of first-century and twenti-eth-century values expands this point (1996, p. 46):

First-century values	Twentieth-century values
Prefers being or being-in-becoming.	Prefers doing.
Prefers collateral or linear relationships.	Prefers individualism.
Focus is on present time.	Focus is on the future.
Humans are subject to nature.	Humans control nature.
Human nature is a mixture of good and evil: evil is expected in this world.	Human nature is good or a mixture of good and evil.

The table demonstrates that the medical values of Europeans and Euro-Americans today, in the main, are very different and even more diverse than those held by the early Christian com-munity from which the Bible was compiled. For first-century people being part of the community was crucial and disability or illness was often a problem as it isolated people from their key relationships. The worldviews of the communally orientated agriculture-based society of the first century is hugely different from the individually orientated, technology-based cultures of the twentieth century. This fact should sound a note of caution to all well-meaning preachers for as Black warns:

> The liberating effects of Jesus' ministry have somehow become lost in the numerous interpretations of these texts over the centuries. The theologies and language used in our sermons affects the disability community in a way that is the reverse of what is intended. (1996, p. 12–13)

Hull vociferously echoes this fact, stating 'many disabled people have come to believe that, far from being a power for their emancipation, the Christian faith is a major source of the social and economic disadvantage that they suffer' (2013, p. 43).

Metaphors

Many issues pertaining to disability – for example, blindness, deafness and lameness – have found their way into the language through metaphorical use. Hull (2013, p. 26) tells us that with regard to blindness the New Testament inherited the legacy that blindness was a punishment from God. This is an area for any preacher or writer to become sensitized to and some scriptures make use of these references. Mostly they depict the impairment as a wilful – and even sinful – choice. In common parlance we may talk of a 'lame excuse' and 'none so blind as those who will not see'. We must note that,

> by not negating the concept that disability is equated with sin, either literally or metaphorically, we as preachers continue to contribute to the alienation of persons with disabilities. Rather than reaching out and embracing them into a healing community of faith. (Black 1996, p. 56)

It is pertinent here that in the famous account in John 9 of the healing of the blind man Jesus states that those who are physically blind have no sin. This of course is said in contrast to the Pharisees who claimed to have insight while refusing to believe the evidence before their eyes. Biblical scholar Louise Lawrence notes:

> Literature on corporeal disease and disability metaphors has attested that incurable ailments were identified as powerful repositories for discourse. The diseased body was frequently used to represent faulty ideologies, practices and politics and belied the schematization of the 'abnormal body' in contrast to the seemingly invisible 'normal' body. (2013, p. 55)

Part of the power of these metaphors is their oversimplification in order to score political points. Lawrence gives the example of 'poverty like a cancer'. Mitchell and Synder point out that disability acts as 'a metaphorical signifier of social and individual collapse' (2000, pp. 47–8). Metaphors are also popular in homiletics on account of their richness. Nevertheless, it is usually at someone's expense. Mostly we are aware these days that the use of black and white as metaphors is detrimental to black, Asian and minority ethnic communities, and here preachers also need to be careful when majoring on images of light and darkness.

Sensory Disability

Perhaps the idiom to turn a blind eye is less offensive, than to be wilfully blind, as it implies more to close the eyes in order not to see, which *is* a volitional matter. Hull urges that metaphors are symptomatic of a certain kind of embodied epistemology (2013, p. 43).

Where we seek to redeem our theology we must also be vigilant about our liturgy as here we can transmit notions even at variance with our teaching. For example the traditional hymn 'Amazing grace' throws up difficulties for some blind people. The triumphant phrase 'I once was blind, but now I see' although symbolic can give the impression that blindness is a pre-Christian state and expected to go when a person comes to faith in Christ. Kathy Black writes about a blind friend of hers who is an African American clergywoman who told her that her response to that hymn is to sing 'I once was blind and still am blind'. Blind theologian John Hull explains why the phrase 'the blind leading the blind' is fallacious as he explains how blind people touch the elbow of the one leading and follow safely in that way. During the days of London smog there was a startling case of sighted people panicking as they failed to see clearly enough to cross the road to return home and being rescued by a blind man who, being accustomed to using different signals to know when the way was clear, led them safely to the other side. In his own experience Hull says that he has often encountered problems when being led by a sighted friend. Department stores are trouble spots for him as the floor may suddenly seem to fall away as his friend leads him into a lift without any prior warning (2013, p. 20). I am in the same league as his sighted friends, as I once led a blind woman cleric astray when attempting to talk her through the food on a buffet table at a disability conference. I wrongly assumed that the little canapés with a chopped deep rose-coloured substance was tomato and told her so. As we sat over lunch she popped one of these in her mouth and declared that the smoked salmon was delicious! I owned up and said that I knew the blind leading the blind was inaccurate but here I was a sighted person and former chef giving her inaccurate information about the food. She said good humouredly 'taste is always the most accurate sense'.

The Bible sometimes indicates hearing as being primary while at other times elevating seeing. For example the Deuteronomic history is often audio-centric while the book of Job is noticeably visiocentric. Famously Job states: 'My ears had heard of you but now my eyes have seen you' (Job 42.5). In the case of Elijah (1 Kings 19) hearing is privileged even over audio-visual theophanies (Avalos 2007, pp. 53–4). It is thought that the emphasis on oralism was an attempt to resist Assyrian and Babylonian influences as power was projected through visual means; Jeremiah also attacks the power of idols (Jer. 10.5).

Sensory disability is an area that throws up some interesting points about how selective our demand for healing can be.

The story goes that a Deaf couple were signing to each other happily when a man approached them and asked if he could pray for them for healing. Regarding themselves, as many Deaf people do, as members of a linguistic minority (sign language users) rather than disabled per se they declined. The man seemed a little dispirited so they called after him if they could pray for him. He hesitated then asked what they wished to pray about and they replied 'for healing for your sight as you wear glasses'.

Deafness and the rise of oralism

The famous *ephphatha* text found in Mark 7.31–37 was at one time used by well-intentioned clergy and educators as 'proof' that it was God's will for people to speech read rather than sign. Harshaw and Black both note that the miracle of the man receiving speech gave rise to a view that in order to be considered fully human and in God's image a person must have speech. This text became one of the foundations of the oralism movement which in many ways was abusive to Deaf people, forbidding them to sign and even forcing them to speak verbally. In this context it must be remembered that Deaf people were understandably reluctant to speak as unintelligible sounds were popularly linked to a lack of intelligence, hence the evolution of the term 'dumb'. Black notes (1996, p. 97) that the edict of the conference of Milan forbade sign language in favour of oralism and Deaf people were duly offended by the lack of understanding of their language and culture displayed by clergy and educators alike; also perhaps the lack of understanding of the eye-strain caused by lip-reading.

One specific area for concern is the notion that hearing is required in order to have faith. John Swinton and Jill Harshaw are clear that faith always originates in God and thus is always a gift from God. Harshaw's perspective is that divine revelation is necessarily attuned to the capacity of the recipient to grasp it.

A further area of concern is where forgiveness and healing have been conflated. Black explains the importance of grasping the way in which the Greek word for healing (*sozein*) was used in the context in which Jesus was operating. The concept of sin in relation to salvation was that *sozein* implied the healing of both the body and the soul: namely forgiveness of sins (Black 1996, p. 113).

Black (p. 118) further clarifies that Mark is more interested in Jesus' ability to forgive sin in the healing narrative of the paralysed man recorded in Mark 2.1–12. As a consequence homileticians have tended also to focus on the issue of forgiveness and thus an oblique view that sin is the cause of the paralysis emerges whether or not it is intentional.

It is important to keep in mind that where there is a clear link between illness and sin it is more often the sin of *another against* a person rather than their own sin, although there are obvious exceptions through negligent or dangerous behaviour. So here if the matter of forgiveness is pertinent it may be in regard to forgiving *another* or indeed, *oneself.*

Mental Illness

Adding to this victim/recipient angle William Barclay (2017, p. 108) in *The Gospel of Luke* offers a thrillingly contemporary interpretation of the healing of the Gadarene demoniac who tells Jesus his name is Legion. Barclay suggests 'it may well be that the word "Legion" haunted him because he had seen atrocities carried out by a Roman Legion when he was a child … which left a scar upon his mind that ultimately sent him mad.' (I am alluding here to the contemporary understanding of PTSD and the impact that we now know trauma can have on a person's mind especially a young person.) The association in this text between what looks like mental illness and the demonic may be a reason why mental illness is still taboo in some countries that believe strongly in demons. Avalos sees signs of hope in the story for us to understand mental illness better. He cites an overlooked aspect of the story as being the long struggle for understanding and life itself among the mentally ill and the fact that this man had coped with a legion of demons that needed a whole herd of pigs to contain them once ejected. He also cites the fact that the community tried to shackle him repeatedly as was the custom until recent times even in Britain. The command 'to go and tell' contrasts strongly with other instances where Jesus forbade those he healed from telling others, and according to Avalos this reveals that the story is vital rather than marginal to the mission and ministry of the gospel (Avalos 2007, p. 142). In conclusion Avalos points out five areas, in this the longest healing narrative in Mark's Gospel, where we are meant to learn and improve our praxis:

- To honour the enormity of the battle of mental illness.
- To create caring communities with strong networks to foster mental health.
- To listen to and tell the stories of struggle and victory with mental illness.
- To show compassion.
- To find the name and numerous commonalities between people regardless of mental status, thus treating them as persons of value. (p. 143)

Ecclesiology and a disablist worldview

In recent years there has been a radical re-examination of ecclesiology for today's world. Some of these writers are themselves impaired or have been powerfully influenced by a loved one with disabilities. They include Amos Yong, Tom Reynolds, Jennie Weiss Block, John Swinton, Henri Nouwen, Jean Vanier, Frances Young, Jill Harshaw, Stanley Hauerwas and Graham Monteith. Others write from a feminist perspective ever mindful of power and justice issues in a church that is often reluctant to challenge the status quo; some of these are Letty Russell, Elizabeth Schüssler-Fiorenza, Serene Jones and Mary Grey. In addition Balkan theologian, Miroslav Volf identifies with much of the feminist egalitarian agenda as he seeks a style of church that can heal divisions. While not offering us an ecclesiology, Nancy Eiseland reframes a traditional under-standing of God positing a 'Disabled God'. Further discussion on this will follow.

Letty Russell in *Church in the Round* (1993) emphasizes relationship and connection aiming to affirm all persons, across all manner of dividing lines. This vision of church endeavours to constantly seek connection, to each other and to justice for those who are oppressed. It is not exclusive in that it concep-tualizes a circle of friendship between world and church by looking for ways in which God is reaching out to those on the margins of both society and church. This sort of theology fits with the concept of Missio Dei that acknowledges God's spirit at work in the secular world independent of the church, but sees that the church is called to join in. Refreshingly she states that 'the ultimate goal of God's household is to do away with the margin and the center by joining the one who is at the center of life in the church but dwells on the margins where he lived and died' (1993, p. 27).

The metaphor of a round table is used to denote a Christian community that practises hospitality. It is non-hierarchical and reflects a biblical image of church found most often in Luke (1993, p.18). Miroslav Volf argues that the church is consti-tuted by the presence of Christ which is mediated through the entire congregation and not simply through its ordained ministers. He states 'the whole congregation functions as mater ecclesia to the children engendered by the Holy Spirit and ... the whole congregation is called to engage in ministry' (1998, p. 2).

In common with some feminist thinkers, Volf rejects the notion of a separative self, preferring to see the self as existing in a web of relationships, always being indwelt by others and itself inhabiting others. Furthermore, he argues for a church where inclusion means nothing less than all members fully participating in formative ways. Volf sees the church as an expression of the Triune God whose essence is personhood.

From the mainstream, Rowan Williams in *Where God Happens* (2005, p. 111) makes the observation that the church is always renewed from the edges and not from the centre. He gives us a definition of a healthy church as one is which we seek to stay connected with God by seeking to connect others with God, one in which we 'win God' by converting one another, and convert one another by our truthful awareness of our frailty. And a church that is living in such a way is the only church that will have anything *different* to say to the world: how deeply depressing if all the church offered were new and better ways to succeed at the expense of others, reinstating the scapegoat mechanisms that the cross of Christ should have exploded once and for all. (2005, p. 27)

Some key disability theologians

Frances Young, writing in *Face to Face* (1990) does not offer us a systematic ecclesiology; her experience of disability through the birth of her first son, Arthur, leads her into a number of spiritual insights some of which are about the church. Furthermore from the trauma and sense of abandonment by God that she experienced at the birth of her profoundly disabled son, she later receives a call to ordained ministry. She believes that belonging to the church depends not on our ability to profess faith (as that would exclude people without speech) but on Christ's acceptance of us. Equally she believes that our own acceptance of one another regardless, is a value to be discovered. She also mounts a challenge to much of our assumed theology. Her experience is that the reality of the birth of her severely disabled son brought conflict with a lot of her own previously held beliefs and the platitudes offered to her by others. She was especially outraged to be told while pregnant with a second baby that she needn't worry as God would not allow the same thing to happen a second time; despite instances of people who have suffered with one child after another while hereditary diseases took hold. Through her three books *Face to Face: A narrative essay on the theology of suffering; Arthur's Call* and *Brokenness and Blessing*, she charts her journey from despair at the birth of her profoundly disabled son, through a lengthy wilderness experience marked by 'a dreadful sense of loss', doubts sapping her energy and wrestling in the dark through to a greater freedom with a sense of deep vocation and the pruning of her theological understanding of the Christian faith (1990, p. 67).

In *Face to Face* she says:

> If we have to abandon some over-simple conceptions in the process, so much the better. It does not necessarily mean we have abandoned Christian belief. We may even have discovered essential insights once central to the faith now submerged by subsequent developments. (1990, p. 55)

She disputes the popular notion that faith automatically gives one the edge in coping with life's problems. She warns that it can lead to delusions or, as in her own case 'it may compound your problems by setting up a sharp dichotomy between an accepted idea of what the world is like and the awful reality of what you actually have to face' (1990, p. 67).

Through the deepening of her faith, she sees that belief and unbelief emerge as two sides of the same coin (1990, p. 135). Drawing on her knowledge of patristics, she refers to Gregory who notes that change is the necessary condition for transformation from glory to glory (2007, p. 19), Cyril – who teaches that we only receive grace as we are obedient and journey to the high country to worship God (2007, p. 22); and finally Origen – who sees that difficulties and even impossibilities are included in the scripture in order to alert us to the fact that the surface reading is inadequate and that deeper meanings need to be teased out. Poignantly she states: 'there is no redemption without the cry of godforsakenness' (1990, p. 137).

> It is this whole complex context that demands that we move beyond an easy spirituality of personal well being, comfort and happiness to rediscover the wilderness way that lies at the heart of the Bible. It is not easy and the challenges are profound. (2007, p. 30)

She warns that the modern mindset believes heaven has been brought to earth. 'We expect Utopia now; if only we can find the right formula, everything can be put to rights' (2007, p. 70).

There is no soft soap in her approach and in common with Henri Nouwen she sees that the way of healing is through wounding and the trajectory of faith is one of *kenosis,* self emptying and downward social mobility:

> yet the wound of love is exactly what heals us. The way of Jesus involves self-emptying, and it is when we can allow 'the other', 'the stranger', those who are different, to challenge our self-sufficiency that we learn what it means to be his disciples. So a biblical spirituality necessitates openness, receptivity and mutuality. (2007, p. 125)

Tom Reynolds, who has a child with multiple disabilities, also gains the insights of an insider position. In common with a number of disablist theologians (Vanier, Nouwen, Hauerwas, Swinton) Reynolds believes that disability offers a profound challenge to our value system and confronts us with some of the less palatable facts of being human. He and his wife know first-hand what it feels like to be misunderstood in the church community. His beautifully written book *Vulnerable Communion* (2008) is a call to hospitality and the warm embrace of God at the heart of Christian faith.

Amos Yong, a Pentecostal theologian who has a brother with Downs syndrome, writing in *Theology and Down syndrome* (2007) also challenges the cult of normalcy.

A significant contribution that Yong makes is in his formulation of a 'pneumatological imagination'. This concept is drawn from the biblical narrative in Acts 2. Yong (p. 11) argues that the many tongues at Pentecost signify both the universality of the gospel message and its capacity to impact the ethnic, linguistic and cultural diversity existing in our world. Yong sees its significance as threefold: raising questions about the one in relation to the many; providing a theological rationale for safeguarding the integrity of difference and otherness; and finally offering an invitation to listen to the plurality of voices in the hope of hearing the voice of the Spirit of God speaking through the 'strange tongues'.

The pneumatological imagination urges us to discern the voice of the Spirit in unlikely contexts, and with this perspective we are also encouraged to discern God's voice through people with learning disabilities as members of the body of Christ. In his ecclesiology he moves towards a church that is not only relevant to disability but is actually constituted by the experience of disability.

Jill Harshaw, in *God Beyond Words,* shaped from her doctoral thesis, fleshes out her theology with all she has learned in raising a profoundly intellectually disabled daughter who does not have speech. In wishing to clarify the often vague and even ambiguous term 'spirituality' she expresses her preference for the term 'spiritual experience' to connote a life-giving encounter and on-going relationship with God (2016, p. 11). Further, in seeking to define the term 'profound intellectual disability' Harshaw offers three agreed criteria across a range of domains: significant impairment of intellectual functioning; significant impairment of social functioning; onset before adulthood.

Theory of accommodation

Drawing on the theory of accommodation which informs us that human capacity is not the determinant issue in the divine/human relationship, Harshaw concludes that the experience of God is also accessible to those who have no cognitive capacities for linguistically based comprehension.

> the fundamental aim of accommodation is relational communication between God and human beings ... words are merely signs and pointers to a reality which is behind and transcends the means of its expression. The person of Jesus Christ is the greatest accommodation to humanity's inability to apprehend God! (2016, p. 115)

Accommodation theory is not simply a tool for divine revelation but perhaps even more wonderfully is a confirmation and sign of the degree to which God aches to communicate and be in relationship with *all* the people he has lovingly made. Gregory of Nyssa goes further and argues that God may not even choose to use language at all. For God's power being

> Exalted far above our nature and inaccessible to all approach [God] like a tender mother who joins in the inarticulate utterances of her babe, gives to our human nature what it is capable of receiving. (2016, p. 106)

Harshaw is emphatic that to claim that God cannot reveal Godself to persons who lack capacity for speech is to limit the ability of God for self-revelation. Harshaw grounds us firmly, insisting that God's accommodation is not verbal but relational, not a proposition but a person (2016, p. 114).

Baptist and disability writer Faith Bowers, who has a son with Downs syndrome, objects to our elevating of linguistic modes of communication and confronts us with the fact that although the word became flesh, ever since we have been trying to turn it back into words! (see Bible Society booklet).

Norris sounds a timely warning here reminding us that 'enfleshed human beings do not have the capacity to grasp God's nature except in faithful acceptance of the mystery' (1991, p. 112).

Stanley Hauerwas, ethicist and theologian, has advocated for people with developmental disabilities since the 1970s. Uniquely within mainstream theology, he has continually and vociferously taken a stand with and for people with disabilities. His starting point is a concern with the nature of being human and how to live this out within the context of the coming kingdom. He disturbs our worldview at both personal and socio-political levels. He calls us to engage with the paradigm shift that began in the life, death and resurrection of Jesus Christ and challenges us within the church to live out and embody this reality. Berkman and Cartwright (2001, p. 4) state 'it is in the wrestling with this process of embodying and living out the gospel that Hauerwas finds genuine revelation in the lives of people with developmental disabilities'. In Chapter 6 we will come across Hauerwas again in the context of his dictum 'to eliminate the disability means to eliminate the subject', which appears to be at the heart of the dispute between Amos Yong and Ryan Mullins.

Models of God for disability inclusion

Jennie Weiss Block and Kathy Black offer images that are inclusive of all – Block with the 'Accessible God' and Black with the 'interdependent God'. Block argues for a theology of access based on the gospel of Jesus Christ being a gospel of access. In *Copious Hosting* she claims that 'creating access for those on the margins is a Christian mandate' (Block 2002, p. 120). Black's concept of the interdependent God resonates with all that has been said about a Trinitarian God.

Following Placher (see Chapter 4) I would add: the 'Vulnerable God' as a fully inclusive and thoroughly Christological motif for disability or rather for all humanity. This also chimes with the work of Thomas Reynolds in *Vulnerable Communion* and with Mary Owen.

Diverse and impairment-specific images of God

Post-modernism, despite gifting us with a renewed awareness of the value of diversity and those on the margins, has robbed us of any sense of such a thing as truth. So if a person who is a redhead has experienced assaults on their self-esteem on account of being ginger they have the right to assert that Jesus was a redhead despite this being in contradiction to what we know of hair colour and ethnicity among Middle Eastern Jews. Presumably it is also feasible to claim that Jesus was a woman for the same reasons. A number of issues need separating here: one is the need to engage with the social and phenomenological aspects of a person's lived experience, a factor of which is often stigma and rejection, the other relates to ontological claims about Jesus. We need to distinguish between the historical Jesus (or Son of Man) who had particularity as a man born in a specific time and place, and Jesus as God (Son of God) or perhaps what Franciscan Richard Rohr among others calls the 'cosmic Christ', who is able to identify and feel with humankind universally. Swinton takes up the problem with impairment specific images of God:

> The danger here is that we end up with a form of theology that is as exclusive as the theology it is trying to replace or challenge, or we find ourselves lost in a mass of impairment-specific God images which may do political work but end up deeply theologically confusing. (2011, p. 285)

The disability literature has some very moving accounts of people with impairments who had an epiphany when they saw Christ with their impairment and this healed them of the pain and sense of stigma they had known. In a Bible Society booklet called *The Bible in Transmission* (2004) on disability, in three separate articles it was evident that there is a clear relationship between a real epiphany and an openness of heart. Professor John Hull writes about the way in which Jesus uses blindness as an insult and speaks through typical ways that sighted people speak to sighted others. He quotes Jesus saying 'Blessed is he [sic] who does not take offence' (Matt. 11.6). He questions how it is possible not to take offence when his experience of life is not acknowledged or validated. Nevertheless, one senses the resistance in him to letting this understandable offence take root in his heart although he rejects the sighted assumptions that Jesus demonstrates in common with the culture of his day.

Later he tells of how touched he was by a revelation of Jesus as his 'blind brother' when Jesus was blindfolded before the crucifixion and provoked when he could not see his tormentors and also of a sense that Jesus may have experienced blindness again when the sky darkened while he was on the cross and he cried out in godforsakenness. Having challenged the ableist assumption that the blind cannot lead the blind, he goes on to celebrate the fact that he now follows Jesus his 'blind brother' who knows the way and so he gently touches his elbow to follow and that they have not got into difficulty yet. For Hull this revelation of Jesus as his 'blind brother' brought him into a closer communion with his Lord.

Two other testimonies in this booklet underline the sense that if we can keep our hearts open, despite the absence of easy answers, the Lord can eventually bring 'shalom'. Nancy Eiesland, author of 'Encountering the Disabled God', and wheelchair user talks of her own special epiphany when she visualized God in a sip puff (breath powered wheelchair) and felt God's identification with her as a person with an impairment. Faith Bowers, Baptist speaker, activist and co-founder of Build whose son has Downs syndrome, speaks of the pain she bore every day of his first 25 years until one day she attended a passion play in which Jesus was played by a man with Downs. When she saw the Downs features contorted in pain on the cross she saw Christ as a person with Downs and she says from that moment the pain left her.

In my view, it is not necessary, even if it were helpful, to claim that God is blind, a person with Downs or a wheelchair user, or any other expression of human diversity. As Hebrews 4.15 states 'we do not have a high priest who is unable to feel sympathy for our weaknesses'. The point is that God loves and accepts us and identifies with our human frailties through the incarnated life he lived and died as a mortal being.

Christian doctrines and disability

In dealing with the issue of ontology we will pick up on the doctrinal issue of eschatology and the resurrection body which is a moot point in the disability debate.

Pentecostal theologian Amos Yong has reformulated some core Christian doctrines to accommodate a disability perspective. From the position of seeing that the basic framework needs overturning he reconceptualizes a number of theological categories: creation, providence, the Fall, what it means to be human, death and resurrection, ecclesiology, eschatology and salvation as a start to reconceptualising the whole. He argues that Christian theological reflection and praxis can be renewed when the traditions and doctrines of the church, which have not been aware of disability issues, are brought into dialogue with disability perspectives. Yong's objective is to enable the formation of suitable Christian attitudes and responses to the experience of disability in late modernity.

He and other theologians, such as Thomas Reynolds, have first-hand experience of disabled relatives and write from a fully engaged insider perspective. Some other theologians have taken issue with them and there was a rich debate published in the *Journal of Religion and Disability*: original article by Ryan Mullins (2011) in *Ars Disputandi* vol. 11(1) and response from Amos Yong (2012) in vol. 12(1).

Downs syndrome in the Resurrection

In the *Ars Disputanti* correspondence during 2011–12, between Amos Yong and Ryan Mullins, a number of key points are in dispute. Yong and Mullins have in common that they both had a sibling with Down syndrome/trisomy 21. Yong claims that it is not feasible for this same person to be resurrected without the continuity of the trisomy 21 element. As they tussle over this issue Mullins takes Yong to task for underpinning his argument with a dictum of the ethicist Stanley Hauerwas namely that 'to eliminate the disability means to eliminate the subject'. Yong later clarifies that his argument stands irrespective of Hauerwas' dictum. Mullins is concerned that the issue of identity has been misconceived:

> It seems to me that Yong has a case of mistaken identity. By this I mean he has confused metaphysical identity with a sense of self. Further, he has confused the 'is' of predication with the 'is' of identity. Necessarily a person is identical with herself. Necessarily a disability is something a person has and not something a person is. (2011, p. 27)

There are other issues raised by Mullins that Yong also takes issue with in response. I will mention one other as it is useful to our purposes here. Returning to the contention of Hauerwas' dictum Mullins objects that this has implications for medical research and how we view the healing narratives of the ministry of Jesus. It has already been noted in the review of the social model that disability activists do not resist medical advances for disability issues, for example cochlear implants. However, in our historical review of the healing miracles of Jesus we did find a highly negative view of the work of Jesus (as expressed, for example by Sharon Betcher) and here we will need to contemplate this matter further.

Mullins states:

> Typically one might look at the gospels and say along with J. B. Green that 'healing is a sign of the inbreaking kingdom of God, reminding the reader that behind the healing ministry of Jesus and others stands Yahweh the healer'. Not so if we take Hauerwas' dictum seriously. The gospels portray Jesus as healing illnesses and curing disabilities ... Jesus is eliminating people left and right in the gospels ... which would seem to call into question the moral character of Jesus and make one sceptical if Yahweh is in fact standing behind Jesus. (2011, p. 28)

We will now move on from the debate between Yong and Mullins which is well worth reading in full. While Mullins seems disturbed by some of Yong's points, he is broadly supportive. He concludes, 'I agree with Yong that Christian thought and practice need to be reformulated precisely because persons with disabilities do have inherent value, and the hope of Christ is for everyone whether they are abled or disabled' (2011, p. 30).

We will now return to the issue of the resurrected body as philosopher, Terrence Ehrman, offers us more light on the subject. In his paper 'Disability and Resurrection Identity', Ehrman also has some arguments with Yong and other disability theologians. His objection is that many of these theologians do not offer an anthropology to support their conclusions about the body in the eschaton. However, he does note that Yong is an exception as he offers an emergentist anthropology 'in which the soul is the emergent form of the body shaped by social and environmental relations'.

Yong, along with some others, is also clear that in the resurrection Jesus bears the marks of his crucifixion:

> Hence the marks of our disabilities continue precisely in order to bear witness to the gloriously redemptive work of God, but now without the physical pain or the social stigma associated with the 'normal' convention of this world's wisdom. (2012, p. 6)

Yong's argument for the continuation of Downs syndrome in the life to come is similarly motivated, all about the glory of God. In *Theology and Down Syndrome* he remarks that redemption for people with Downs syndrome 'will not consist in some magical fix of the twenty-first chromosome but in the recognition of their central roles both in the communion of saints and in the divine scheme of things.'

> Christian hope of resurrection requires that the one raised be the same person who died. Many theologians now argue that disability is essential to identity and thus cannot be eliminated in the life to come. Ehrman argues that a Thomist Hylemorphic anthropology provides the best context to understand the human person so that disability is not essential to identity. Ehrman surely rightly asserts that 'in the resurrection we shall become truly ourselves'. (2007, p. 282)

For a fuller understanding of the argument I refer the reader to the full article, but here I shall state the argument in its simplest form. To offer a solution that sits better with classical theology but takes disability issues seriously he offers a Thomist hylemorphist anthropology (don't lose me now – it is in the Glossary) which presents the human being as a unified psycho-physical whole and which can account for the dignity of every person as the imago Dei and maintain diachronic resurrection identity (Ehrman 2015, p. 727). In this view 'the soul is the organizing principle of the body and not just a 'pilot in the ship' as Plato thought (p. 729). Here at last we have a rationale that does not require us to argue one way or the other and this is crucial as with this area it is clear that for some Yong's view could strip them of their hope for life in the resurrection. It is surely our pastoral concern to do no such thing.

Liberation Theologies of Disability

A number of authors have drawn from liberation theology, with its focus on freedom for the poor and social justice for all. Hannah Lewis writes a Deaf liberation theology and Jane Wallman uses it for her work on blindness. However, L'Arche challenges liberation theology, on the basis that the 'poverty' of people with learning disabilities cannot be removed. It also reminds us of the limits of the human capacity to 'put things right' (Young 2014, p. 94).

Nancy Eiseland in 'Encountering the Disabled God' also offers a liberation theology of disability. Eiseland (2004) perhaps goes further than many others in that she sees God as a wheelchair user, like herself, as that is how God has revealed himself to her. While this vision offers solidarity to believers with disabilities (or maybe just wheelchair users) it does not go unchallenged even among disablist theologians such as Yong who questions whether as a metaphor it may not actually distort our view of God. Deborah Creamer (2004) is concerned that this view does nothing to help those who struggle with ambivalent feelings about their disabilities (and we must remember here that there is no one singular experience of disability) and Hinkle (2003) doubts the utility of applying this concept to a God who is intellectually disabled. Yong concludes that Eiseland's theology of a disabled God is valuable in that it foregrounds 'God's embracing the full range of the human condition in the incarnation so as to insist on a truly liberative and inclusive community of faith – it is limited as, an only, or even, dominant model, for contemporary disability theology and Christology' (2007, p. 176). Mary Owen, American disability rights activist, philosopher, policy expert and writer rejects the concept of a disabled God as the concept of the wounded Christ has caused discord among the Disability Rights Movement. She states (1993) that those who are Christians are the Easter people so identify more with their gifts than with their brokenness.

Before moving on we will return to a discussion of Eiseland's disabled God. Although such a concept seems radical and strange, the idea is not new and was, in fact, first propounded by theologian Alan Lewis in 1983 in an article entitled 'God as cripple: disability, personhood and the reign of God'. In this he argues that Jesus, the healer, had become the 'cripple' (sic), despised, rejected, weakened with the afflictions of others, sick with their diseases, and for them disfigured by an ugliness (as of some archetypal Elephant man?) from which faces are turned away (Isa. 53.3) (1983, p. 17). To us the notion of a disabled God is very challenging but no more so than a crucified God was in Jesus' own day. Martin Albl tells us, 'in the ancient world, a crucified person was the ultimate example of "disability". On the one hand, the crucified person was the ultimate symbol of "functional limitations" … and on the other "of social stigmatization".' It may well be that in our age we need this new image that shocks us in ways that a crucified God does not, on account of the image having been domesticated over time. Albl concludes: 'Paul completely reverses standard categories of thought, speaking of the "foolishness"' and "weakness" of the ultimate source of wisdom, strength and power' (2007, p. 150).

Contextual Theology

A note on contextual theology might be helpful here. Stephen Bevans defines contextual theology as:

A way of doing theology in which one takes into account the spirit and message of the gospel; the tradition of the church; the culture in which one is theologizing; and social change within that culture, whether brought about by western technological process or the grass-roots struggle for equality, justice and liberation. (1992, p. 1)

Disability theology launches a challenge to some classical interpretations of such topics as eschatology. While some stalwarts object to new interpretations as representing a drift from 'pure' theology, contextual theology makes plain that all theology is contextual and maybe some classical theologians are failing to see the bias in their own received viewpoint. Yuzon (1992, p. 3) points out that the theology of Thomas Aquinas is a response to the Aristotelean worldview, and the hierarchical framework of the world. The crisis theology of Karl Barth was born out of the reality of World War One and disenchantment with liberal theologies.

The strength of contextual theology lies in its recognition of the vital importance of human experience as a starting point for reflection on matters of faith and morality. A further strength is that it speaks to specific contexts and as such does not expect its interpretations to be unchanging or generalizable in a normative fashion. Classical theology appeals to scripture and tradition and may pride itself on being unchanging over time. However, while a purely 'objective/outsider' vantage point may seem to some to be better, we should note that God Godself does not operate on that basis and Jesus Christ came in the flesh in order to take an extraordinary insider position to fathom the human condition. Yuzon notes, 'if the church is to touch people's lives with God's message in a meaningful way it must communicate that message incarnationally' (1992, p. 2). A further strength is that it embodies a view of reality as holistic rather than compartmentalized.

Points for Discussion and/or Reflection

1 Has this chapter introduced you to a more complex view of handling scripture? If so, do you welcome or reject it?
2 What is your response to the debate between Amos Yong and Ryan Mullins regarding how people with Downs syndrome will be in the afterlife?
3 Did the argument that people who lack speech can have a relationship with God surprise you? Did it contradict something you had been taught before?

References

Albl, M. (2007), '"For wherever I am weak then I am strong", Disability in Paul's Epistles', in Avalos, H., Melcher, S. and Schipper, J. (eds), *This Abled Body: Rethinking Disabilities in Biblical Studies*, Atlanta: Society of Biblical Literature.

Avalos, H., Melcher, S. and Schipper, J. (2007) (eds), *This Abled Body: Rethinking Disabilities in Biblical Studies*, Atlanta: Society of Biblical Literature.

Barclay, W. (2017), *Gospel of Luke*, Westminster: John Knox Press.

Berkman, J. and Cartwright, M. (2001), *The Hauerwas Reader*, North Carolina: Duke University Press.

Bevans, S. (1992), *Models of Contextual Theology*, New York: Orbis Books.

Bible Society (2004), 'Disability and the image of God', in *The Bible in Transmission*, Spring.

Black, K. (1996), *A Healing Homiletic*, Nashville: Abingdon Press.

Bowers, F. (2004), 'Who sinned?', in 'Disability and the image of God', *The Bible in Transmission*, Spring, The Bible Society.

Creamer, D. (2004), 'The withered hand of God: disability and theological reflection', *PhD thesis*, Iliff School of Theology and the University of Denver (Colorado Seminary)

Eiseland, N. (2004), 'Encountering the Disabled God', in 'Disability and the image of God', *The Bible in Transmission*, Spring, The Bible Society.

Ehrman, T. (2015), 'Disability and Resurrection Identity', Phil papers.

Fritzon, A. and Kabue, S. (2004), *Interpreting Disability: A Church of All and for All*, Geneva: Risk Book.

Harshaw, J. (2016), *God Beyond Words*, London: Jessica Kingsley.

Hinkle, C. (2003), 'Smart enough for the church? Liberal Protestantism and cognitive disability'. Paper presented at the American Academy of Religion.

Hull, J. (2013), *The Tactile Heart*, London: SCM Press.

Lawrence, L. (2013), *Sense and Stigma in the Gospels*, Oxford: OUP.

Lewis, A. (1983), 'God as cripple: disability, personhood and the reign of God' in *Pacific Theological Review* 16(11), pp. 13–18.

Mitchell, D. and Synder, S. (2000), *Narrative Prosthesis: Disability and the Dependencies of Discourse*, Michigan: University of Michigan.

Monteith, G. (2005), *Deconstructing Miracles*, Glasgow: Covenanters Press.

Mullins, R. T. (2011), 'Some Difficulties for Amos Yong's Disability Theology of the Resurrection', in *Ars Disputandi* vol. 11(1).

Norris, F. (1991), *Faith Gives Fullness to Reasoning: The Five Theological Orations of Gregory of Nazanzien*, trans. Wickham, L. and Williams, F., Leiden: Brill.

Owen, M. (1993), 'Frayed at the edges: The intertwined threads of life and disability'. Respect Life Program, Washington D.C. United States Catholic conference.

Reynolds, T. (2008), *Vulnerable Communion*, Michigan: Brazos Press.

Russell, L. (1993), *Church in the Round*, Kentucky: Westminster/John Knox Press.

Swinton, J. (2001), 'A Church for Strangers' in *JRDH* 4(4), pp. 25–63.

Volf, M. (1998), *After our Likeness: The Church as the Image of the Trinity*, Grand Rapids: Eerdmanns.

Weiss Block, J. (2002), *Copious Hosting*, New York and London: Continuum.

Williams, R. (2005), *Where God Happens*, Boston: New Seeds.

Yong, A. (2007), *Theology and Down Syndrome*, Texas: Baylor University Press.

Yong, A. (2012), 'Disability Theology of the Resurrection: Persisting Questions and Additional Considerations. Response to R. T. Mullins', in *Ars Disputandi* vol. 2(1).

Yong, A. (2014), *Ars Disputandi* vol. 12.

Young, F. (1990), *Face to Face: A narrative essay in the theology of suffering*, Edinburgh: T & T Clark.

Young, F. (2007), *Brokenness and Blessing*, London: Darton Longman and Todd.

Young, F. (2014), *Arthur's Call*, London: SPCK.
Yuzon, L. (1992), 'Towards a Contextual Theology', *CTC Bulletin*.

Further Reading

Critical reflections on Stanley Hauerwas' *Theology of Disability: disabling society, enabling theology*, John Swinton (ed.), 2004, Haworth Pastoral Press: London: New York.
For a fuller exploration of embodiment see chapter 3 of Deborah Creamer's (2012), *Disability and Christian Theology*.

Summary

In this chapter we have explored the role of hermeneutics in biblical interpretation, and we have highlighted some key issues for preachers and homileticians. Difficulty with the use of metaphors was foregrounded in the context primarily of sensory disability, and here we looked at the varied importance placed on hearing or sight in the scriptures. A brief consideration of mental illness was presented in the context of Mark's story of the Gadarene 'demoniac'. Ecclesiology was then discussed within the context of a disability worldview and some key disability theologians were presented. Jill Harshaw's work on people with profound disabilities and no speech was explored and the theory of accommodation with regard to God's revelation was outlined. Models of God for disability inclusion were examined and the use of liberation theology for disability issues was noted. Finally, we moved into the most complex area where Christian doctrines are debated and reformulated in the light of disability awareness. A brief introduction to contextual theology was given to help readers navigate this territory. A doctrine that is particularly contentious is that of the resurrection body and the question of whether identity depends on continuity in the next life. Discussion here centres on the case of people with Downs syndrome, and whether or not they will have Downs in the life to come. A debate between two theologians, Amos Yong and Ryan Mullins, both with a close relative who had Downs syndrome, was introduced and revealed a hotly contested domain. Some helpful philosophical insights from Terrence Ehrman were brought into the discussion enabling us to avoid a categoric verdict on this issue.

6

The Contemporary Scene for Disability and the Church

Moves Towards Inclusion

For the church the introduction of the Disability Discrimination Act 2005 (DDA) finally put disability firmly on the agenda, despite the fact that there had been talk of the importance of inclusion in the church for nearly five decades! A declaration of the fourth congress of The World Council of Churches in Cologne in 1968 states that 'Churches without persons with disabilities are disabled churches.' In 1978 a special ecumenical European consultation insisted that when we confess our conviction that all human beings are one in the family of God that we are affirming that no person may be excluded on the pretext of disability.

Bryant and Reynolds have estimated that in an average parish there will be between 10–15 per cent of people with some type of impairment, and note that this is a statistic that is seldom reflected in the constitution of the congregation, and this statistic is currently set nearer to the 20 per cent mark.

The DDA is not merely about physical access to buildings but also includes enjoyment of the use of all the buildings, services and facilities.

Discrimination should also cover 'intellectual access' and Mencap have issued guidelines on accessible language out of which some prayers are now being rewritten. The guidelines state that sentences should be short with only one main idea per sentence, that jargon should be avoided as should abstract concepts including all figurative language. Writing should be in the same style as spoken language and all unnecessary detail should be removed. Finally, and crucially, written texts should be supported by visual images so that the message is clear to readers and non-readers alike. A preacher could helpfully be asked to sum up what has been said in around two sentences for those with learning disabilities.

Some bad practices such as putting an adult person with Downs in the Sunday school with infants because of the 'mental age' have been reviewed.

Those that have a handle on the issues demonstrate that they realize disability is about rights and not charity and about independence and not care. A church policy document that gives the distinct impression that it has been written enthusiastically before sufficient dialogue, states: 'I think we are both loving and caring in our attitude to others, but I'm sure we can help people to feel *even more* welcome' (my emphasis).

In *Open to All*, written by people with extensive experience of working with disabled people, we read on the topic of welcoming:

> It can be very uncomfortable to hear what people with physical, learning, or sensory disabilities or with mental health needs have to say about the church's attitudes towards them but we need to listen and to assure those concerned that they have been heard. (Bryant and Reynolds 2001, p. 29)

This less positive view is confirmed by Canadian Jewish Sociologist Avi Rose, who, in claiming that religious communities are not making the necessary accommodations for people with disabilities, says: 'This fact seems to conflict with the general perception of religious institutions as havens for all peoples' (1997, p. 396). Going one step further the World Council of Churches 'Interim statement', *A Church of all and for all* (2003), written by people with disabilities and those closely involved with disabled people, while acknowledging that there have been some improvements in the past two decades states:

> It is important to be aware that, in some parts of the world and in some churches, there has recently been a return

towards overprotection and even disregard of disabled persons. In some places, we have been manipulated by evangelical groups. Even worse than being ignored, manipulating disabled people could become the Church's new sin. (2003, p. 13, para. 72)

Unless the church changes its modus operandi people with learning disabilities will not be included. Moreover, the *Church Times* stated: 'People with learning disabilities have spiritual needs that are not being met by the Churches' (30 April 2004). This fact is corroborated by a report published by the Foundations for People with learning disabilities. The foundation's chief executive, Andrew McCulloch, insists: 'Faith communities are not always welcoming or inclusive, despite the requirements of the DDA.'

The report insists that the welcome people with learning disabilities receive is at best superficial and stops at the church door as they are not usually invited into people's homes. It would seem then that it is not simply spiritual needs that are left unmet but emotional and social needs. It concludes that the real challenge is for people with learning disabilities to be able to participate in the life of the entire community of believers. In my research work I observed an Anglican church in which this total inclusion and participation was lived out. It was a great inspiration. Two young men with Downs syndrome served communion, their midweek group was given a 'slap-up' dinner every year in common with the other church groups. Members of the congregation knew them by name and spoke lovingly about them. Another church I observed had a lovely couple who did a lot of socializing and some Bible study with those with learning disabilities in their church. They organized exciting themed days out for them and helped to make them feel a part of the church. I think they had an uphill battle with the culture that the rest of the church had bought into, however. It is doubtless a long journey to shift the culture of a church congregation away from valuing the status quo even though the gospel is so clear about the countercultural values of the Kingdom.

In 2009 a church report was produced called 'Opening the Doors: Ministry with People with Learning Disabilities and People on the Autistic Spectrum'. Torch Trust produced fully accessible versions of the report, thus putting into practice some of the recommendations of the report. In the foreword, the Archbishop of York, John Sentamu, writes movingly: 'This is not just another set of official guidelines – it is an invitation to the church to walk on holy ground' (2009, p. 4). The report covers key issues such as: appropriate language, theological rationale for full inclusion of people with learning disabilities, issues for people on the autistic spectrum, dealing with parents and carers and life events that the church must handle, death and bereavement, love and marriage, confirmation and admission to communion.

Reflections on the Disability Movement's Criticisms of the Church

Despite the fact that there are some serious moves afoot to improve the lot of people with impairments in the church, the Disability Movement, frequently asserts that some of the negative experience of disabled people and indeed those who have disabled children, has its origins in some strongly held beliefs about disability in the Judaeo-Christian tradition.

North American disability activists Eiseland (1994) and Majik (1994) object to the insistence that Judaeo-Christian thinking is oppressive towards disabled persons. Canadian sociologist Avi Rose makes a much stronger claim than either of his British counterparts (Barnes and Shakespeare) stating: 'the views of Western religious institutions have helped to create the social construct of disability as a political state of oppression and have been instrumental in maintaining its power and pervasive nature'. The strength of this assertion may reflect some significant differences between the American and British religious contexts.

On the British scene, Barnes (1996) and Shakespeare (1997, p. 228) state that Judaeo-Christian thinking and that of the

Greeks have been detrimental to people with disabilities, and here I would like to reiterate the point that during the Medieval era Christianity was overlaid with Greek thinking to the detriment of the purity of the gospel.

Jewish educator Avi Rose (1997, p. 396), who is especially critical of Judaeo-Christian attitudes, sets out four headings under which disability is viewed:

1 Disability as punishment for sin.
2 Disability as challenge to divine perfection.
3 Disability as incompetence and exemption from religious practice.
4 Disability as object of pity and charity.

Rose admits that the latter category may be double-edged. On the positive side, because both the Talmud and the Bible instruct people to care for those with disabilities, religious institutions were historically the first and sometimes sole providers of care for disabled people. In the forefront of care were religious orders who offered schooling, medical support and charitable funding for the benefit of people with impairments. However, the downside is that being viewed as objects of pity inclines to objectification of the person, a response that leads to an undermining of the person's essential humanity. Rose points out another danger, warning 'they become a project, a vehicle for others to fulfil their acts of kindness'. And this is something I have heard disabled people at conferences express. 'Don't make me your salvation!'

A further drawback to this charitable perspective is that where people become a charitable responsibility, their needs are less likely to be recognized as rights but as privileges of a society that is affluent enough to care for them.

Watson in *Civilisation and the Cripple* asserts that the book of Leviticus (especially chapter 21), with its exclusion from 'offering sacrifices' for people with disabilities, gave credibility to a view of disability as a sign of 'the curse of God'. Such verses became 'clobber texts' – 'a useful stick with which to beat the cripple' (Watson 1930, p. 2). Expanding on this point he states that such an obvious 'curse' as deformity was seen as a sure sign of spiritual corruption.

As we have seen this was true within the Medieval era. Popular stories circulate which are sometimes ascribed to Luther and sometimes the self-same tales are ascribed to Calvin indicating that these people saw disabled children as demonized.

Augustine saw impairment as a punishment for the Fall of Adam and other sins. The Medieval view that a disabled child was 'a changeling', that is, a demonic substitute for a human child as a consequence of sin – more often seen as the fruit of a sexual liaison between the mother and the devil, was set out in the *Malleus Maleficarum* of 1487.

Tension Between the Gospel and the Institutional Church

The tension between the nature of the gospel and the culture of the institutional church is taken up by a number of writers. Wilks and Pestell show concern for the integrity of the gospel when they say: 'where Christians set up a system that does not express this total and perfect equality amongst God's people, we fail to express and live the liberating heart of the Gospel' (2003, p. 4).

Alan Lewis in his prophetic article entitled 'God as Cripple: Disability, personhood and the reign of God' claims

> one of the tests of the credibility and relevance of the gospel is the damage it can inflict upon vicious circles ... The circle of alienation is nowhere more vicious, nor the need for its rupture more urgent, than in our handicapping of the handicapped [sic]. (1983, p. 13)

Numerous writers point out that the gospel itself incorporates a desire for social justice and inclusion for all people. And Lesslie Newbigin insists on the need for the message of the gospel to be grounded in the lived experience of a community:

'the only hermeneutic of the gospel, is a congregation of men and women who believe and live by it' (1989, p. 227).

While it might be thought that some people in the Disability Movement could be antithetical to the church, it must not be assumed that criticisms of the church are to be found solely from outside. Carole Fontaine insists that the church is one of the places in which the most potent examples of exclusion can be experienced (1995, p. 288). She believes this is partly because the presence of disabled believers is an embarrassment to the church's ideology of healing. She concludes 'it is no wonder that churches respond so slowly and ineptly to the special needs of this community, for they are themselves handicapped by their theological legacy' (p. 295).

One writer comments on a tendency within evangelical thinking to unconsciously construct a harmonizing gloss on the scriptures which obscures the unique perspective of the many different writers.

The late, blind theologian professor, John Hull, gives us a different take on this same point:

> If there is an absolute truth, it is not to be found through a process of artificial and often unconscious absolutizing, but through a proliferation of many meanings, until everyone's meanings are gathered in. This is the way the Bible becomes truly ecumenical, truly catholic. (Hull 2013, p. 15)

Pentecostal theologian Amos Yong states starkly: 'the complaints about Pentecostal-charismatic healing practices are legion in the disability literature' (2007, p. 242). His forthright and important conclusion is that the need is not so much for disabled people to be healed as for non-disabled people to be transformed and, indeed, for all persons to have their conceptual lenses, through which people and their bodies are viewed, reground in order to encompass the experience of disability. Yong quotes the experience of Mary Semple who believed that her tumours had been an agent of God to save her from an abusive marriage. This underscores the danger of the tunnel vision that only seeks the person's physical wellbeing. In my own life I have observed the positive impact of a man with major mental health issues losing his hearing as the signing group that he became part of welcomed him more whole-heartedly than I had previously observed among the main congregation. This example again underscores the need for a wider lens through which to view the situation and of course the need to dialogue with the person involved to gain their perspective.

Many people within the church have told painful tales of misunderstandings, sometimes by believers who have the sort of simplistic faith that 'Job's comforters' display. Brett Webb-Mitchell writes from experience within the current western context 'as a person who had some motor difficulties, John, who wanted to be in the church, had a hard time convincing the congregation that he didn't need to be exorcised' (1994, p. 9). John Swinton is also clear that the church is not necessarily a '"safe space" in which to experience acceptance, peace and fellowship with other believers' (2001, p. 35). Featherstone and other parents of children with disabilities talk about the anxiety of a God of retribution who may be punishing them through the deformation of their children for some known or even unknown sin. Frank Daly points out that for many parents whose children were born mentally or physically impaired there are many burdens to bear and the feeling of being rejected by God is one of them.

Frank Daly in Kelly and McGinley (2000) also takes up the issue of parental injury from false views. He states that historically parents took up vehement campaigns for their children to receive Holy Communion:

> They were often met with thinly veiled rebuffs from priests more concerned with canonical exactitude than pastoral care. They were told that this could not be because their children 'did not understand' what Holy Communion was. In one dreadful case, a loving mother who nursed her son for 29 years to his death was told that, 'it would be like giving it to a dog'. (Kelly and McKinley 2000, p. 13)

They explain that such priests and pastors fail to see that for these parents being welcome to receive the Lord at Holy Communion, crucially, meant that the church and God welcomed their child as a human being and a full person.

Another negative response found within the church could be called 'disability as inappropriate'. John Swinton writes of the alienating experience in taking a young man with Downs syndrome to a local church. They were given a stark ultimatum: either to send the young man (not a child) to the Sunday school or leave! Understandably they chose the latter option. Swinton remarks: 'in the name of "orthodoxy", "right worship" and "fairness to other worshippers"', the church felt justified in excluding Stephen from the worshipping community' (2001, p. 42).

Webb-Mitchell (1994) is surely right in saying that our perceptions of others are learned in the culture we are raised in and, in fact, significantly shape our attitude towards all people, regardless of ability or disability.

Having looked at some of these failings I will introduce some very refreshing work going on in some sectors of the church in the western world.

Recent Initiatives

Parachurch ministries for people with learning disabilities

The first steps to make room for people with disabilities came with the founding of a number of ministries for people with learning disabilities that operate alongside the local church. We shall look at Causeway Prospects, SPRED, Faith and Light and L'Arche.

Causeway Prospects was founded in 1976 by David and Madeleine Potter as 'A Cause for Concern'. It is a voluntary Christian organization which exists to support people with learning disabilities in order to help them enjoy a full life. It has very clearly defined values which include individuality, empowerment, dignity, independence, inclusion and spirituality with a strong emphasis on the individual's right to autonomy and self-determination in all matters concerning their lives. Tony Phelps-Jones sees it as a mission to people with learning disabilities in order for them to know that Jesus loves them. Groups meet for regular prayer, Bible study and friendship. Holidays and regional celebrations are also available. Causeway Prospects provides training and advice for churches on effective ministry and outreach.

SPRED stands for Special Religious Development and was formed in the 1960s in Chicago as a response to the fact that the church was not teaching faith in ways that worked for people with learning disabilities. They meet either weekly or bi-weekly, share food and listen to the Word together and take part in activities. It is based on the parish system thus enabling members to be linked to a parish church.

According to their webpage 'The goal of SPRED is to assist people in parish churches to integrate persons with a learning disability into parish life and worship through the process of education in faith.'

Faith and Light is part of the Roman Catholic Church. It was founded in the 1970s and grew out of a pilgrimage to Lourdes which was run by Jean Vanier who also founded the L'Arche communities. At Easter 1968, in response to the needs of one family, a group of 8,000 people from a total of 15 countries took part in a pilgrimage to spend Easter together. These groups, on their return, became the first Faith and Light communities, giving support to families who had members with learning disabilities and who had experienced rejection and isolation in the church. To date there are over 1,500 communities in 85 countries, and these include people from a variety of Christian traditions. They meet monthly for worship, activities and simply for friendship. Larger events also take place, including retreats and celebrations as they are members of an ecclesial and international organization. Unlike L'Arche, Faith and Light are not residential communities.

L'Arche communities are well known as they are a worldwide concern for people of a variety of faith traditions and of none. Originally they were a Roman Catholic concern established by Jean Vanier and a French priest. They have been in existence for over 40 years (there are now 130 around the world) but these are residential communities where non-disabled people live in community with people with learning disabilities. Inspiration has been drawn from the writings of both Jean Vanier and the late Dutch priest and academic Henri Nouwen. L'Arche has a value system that seeks to honour the uniqueness of each person and the right and need of every person to give and receive love and friendship and to grow spiritually. They are quite distinct from any other work with people with learning disabilities as they are residential and aim for non-disabled people to live and work alongside people with intellectual impairments. Because they are a burgeoning organization and have been going for some time, some research has already been conducted on them. One example of such is the ethnographic research of American pastor Brett Webb-Mitchell, who lived at L'Arche, Lambeth for nine months in 1987–88 while conducting ethnographic research.

Webb-Mitchell's findings are not quite so unambiguous as the accounts we read from Jean Vanier and others. He writes that the theme of L'Arche as a ghetto was a new theme to him before embarking on his research (1988, p. 44). He finds that at times L'Arche seems no different from any other institution he had worked in with people with learning disabilities. He points out that there are no plans for anyone to move beyond L'Arche towards independence. One local church leader noted that the L'Arche people do not participate in the life of the local church very much as they are too busy with things at L'Arche. Webb-Mitchell recommends that L'Arche follows the rest of England in focusing on a developmental approach. He feels that L'Arche has become stuck in 'being' while the rest of society is focusing on 'becoming'. He also sees that becoming is more conducive to participation. On the topic of participation he observes during a two-day celebration that the people with learning disabilities are only included as 'side-kicks' in the drama and liturgy and that they are not able to participate in attending their case reviews. The data also raises some questions over how much choice the residents at L'Arche have in their personal lives. On balance, he concludes that L'Arche has more characteristics of an institution than a community.

Further, noting that members of L'Arche do not take much part in the local church, he wonders if it is time for them to participate more fully in the life of the church rather than creating a substitute for church. In this vein he suggests that it may be time for L'arche (the ark) to get out of *their* ark and join the rest of the church.

Aside from these separate ministries for people with learning disabilities some people are now beginning to establish churches specifically for this constituency.

Fresh Expressions of church for people with learning disabilities

Claire Dalpra researched two new expressions of church and wrote about them in the Church Army pamphlet *Encounters on the Edge no 44: Hidden treasures*. This is a move beyond forming a separate group to then feed in to a regular congregation. It is a separate church designed to be appropriate to that specific culture.

Fenland Community Church in March, Cambridgeshire, meets behind the Sainsbury superstore in a scout hall, thrice monthly. Chairs are set in a semi-circle, two or three rows deep which is flexible for wheelchair users. The floor is marked for ball games so ambience is not as good as location. The superstore car park is useful for dropping off and picking up and also for carers to do some shopping while they wait. The service is described as 'fun, interactive, fairly noisy and active time of worship' (lots of people wandering around) lasting about an hour. Claire Dalpra made the following observations. Sometimes a person with learning disabilities opens in prayer with a little help from the pastor. Simple songs from Causeway Prospects and modern choruses are led by the worship leader on guitar and the leader uses Makaton signing. They aim to use songs with as little imagery as possible and percussion instruments and flags are available for anyone to use. They use the visual too and during the songs the leader's wife imaginatively wraps large sheets of soft material around members who are unable to move or see to encourage a sense of inclusion (being joined together by the fabric). At one point a large number of people dance in the middle and others wave ribbons and flags.

A time of confession is conducted with the use of stones which are handed round and used to symbolize things we do wrong which could then be brought to the front and laid at the foot of the cross. Objects were often handed round: wooden crosses, candles, flowers and so on. Visual images were projected on to the screen to reinforce what was being said so that words did not have to stand alone. There was also some storytelling with puppets.

Their church logo is a picture of a bruised reed, communicating something of the difficulty that many of their members have experienced in engaging with society outside the learning disability community.

Another example of fresh expressions is a church in Sheffield, St Paul's Norton Lees, which rents a space for fortnightly evening worship called Focus. The church is described as a mix of old and new with stained glass windows and carpeting and well-lit areas with flexible seating. The team use alternate Sundays for planning, perhaps an indication of the labour intensity of this ministry.

Focus begins with worship and volunteers bringing in the cross and lighting the candles. Use of musical instruments and key phrases like 'we're God's family' are repeated. Interactive drama is a main feature. The leader takes the role of narrator and members of the congregation volunteer to act out key parts with simple costume and props and the repetition of lines from the narrator.

Prayer needs are identified pictorially on a flip chart and then prayed for with some assistance from those who had identified the needs. The service concludes with a light supper and there is cake to honour any birthday that had taken place. Once transport arrives the meeting breaks up and people are taken home.

Although there are a number of similarities between these

two groups, there are also sufficient differences to establish that each is finding its unique way within the prevailing culture of disability without merely aping what someone else has pioneered. Claire Dalpra states: 'the instinct to grow what seems appropriate to the local context rather than pre-determining a framework ahead of time seems alive and well' (2009, p. 15).

Despite being very intentional in what they do, the leaders seem settled with the idea of Focus as a provision for people with learning disabilities as an expression of church in isolation from the rest of the church. Dalpra explains that having moved to Sheffield David looked for possibilities to nurture adults with learning disabilities and came to the rather ableist conclusion (my judgement not Dalpra's) that 'it was unreasonable to expect an ordinary church to change the fundamentals of how they do church in order to accommodate the needs of a few people in their congregations with learning disabilities'.

However, they rightly point out how ill-equipped the average church is to run such a ministry and note that many so-called 'learning disabled-friendly' churches still have sermons that are just monologues and little or no understanding of cognitive human development theory. Even with expertise their own team have difficulty communicating a simple message through action and getting it right every time. Dalpra concludes: 'they are also keen to note that the wider church explores the theological implications of engagement with this mission context to avoid ministry that is fuelled by mere sympathy vote or token gesture' (2009, p. 13).

After her visits to these two churches Dalpra considers to what extent they fulfil the criteria for a fresh expression of church. She notes that the first aspect which is crucial is an instinct for enculturation rather than mere assimilation. In view of this priority she was interested that the leaders of the Cambridgeshire church called themselves cross-cultural missionaries to a lost tribe. Focus has two members on their leadership team who take an active part in the leading of the church by helping to plan the services. They realize that there is also a need to include an awareness of what carers need in this sort of church that can avoid making it 'a busman's holiday'

(2009, p. 24). Carers play a key part as they build connections into residential homes which can otherwise be a closed world. Dalpra concludes, 'these stories tell of Christians living a delightfully counter-cultural stance' (p. 29).

Regarding inclusion Dalpra notes:

> I discovered that the leaders of *Focus* believe that *having a dedicated church for those with learning disabilities helps members feel more normal* [my emphasis] than they would if they joined a 'normal' church. It is better to have a church that takes the learning disabled seriously with the freedom to address the particular issues in their culture. Choice is a big issue for them in that very often they have had precious little. Focus tries to give it back by offering as much choice as they responsibly can at every meeting. (p. 6)

The danger of attending but not belonging is guarded against through emphasis on regular attendance. Knowing everyone's names, giving a genuine welcome, eating together and using an inclusive seating arrangement, all help to create a sense of belonging over a merely passive attendance (p. 18).

While it may be laudable for people to establish churches that are learning-disabled friendly, there are some difficulties with this approach. First the notion that they feel more 'normal' on their own and, more so, that it is not reasonable to expect the church to change its way of doing church. There is a place for specific groups as a first step and a form of consciousness-raising; however, in the final analysis, *together*, we are the Body of Christ.

Causeway Prospects advocate the approach of groups existing within a wider church structure. Dalpra questions how much mutuality there is in that. Her concern over mutuality is based on a pattern she has seen in churches working to integrate middle and working-class cultures and the fact that the more educated group has a tendency to dominate. She notes that the more verbal and intellectual the church tradition is the more difficult this pattern is to break.

Both churches she visited had developed a sacramental

aspect to their services and even written their own liturgy. Communion is chaotic and the notion that a tiny piece of bread is appropriate is not easily comprehensible to many of them.

In writing about the gifts of vulnerable mission Dalpra says:

> I discovered a complex dynamic in which people started as hosts but over time became guests. Vanier describes this as moving from 'doing for them' to 'being with them' that often develops as a permanent vocation to live within the particular culture, in this case the culture of disability. This resonates with insights from our team that connect the cross-cultural missionary as guest to something akin to willing slavery. This is powerful imagery with the New Testament call to servanthood that voluntarily submits itself to the person or the people they are serving. Those leading these churches talked about member's weaknesses unearthing parallel weaknesses in them. (p. 27)

Everyone spoke of the rewarding nature of this ministry.

> Their simplicity and spontaneity of lifestyle is refreshing next to the complexity of many. Furthermore, connecting to the insights of Vanier and Nouwen, there is something about an encounter with a learning disabled person that can more easily lead to an encounter with God. (p. 28)

Traditional forms of church are found to be 'peripheral, obscure, confusing and irrelevant'. Her final conclusion is this:

> We must allow church for the learning disabled space to explore what steps in their journey towards maturity will need to be taken <u>and</u> in what order. In reaching out to others in mission, in gathering enough resources to sustain what they've started and in searching for ways of expressing a catholicity built on mutual appreciation, we, the so-called 'able' have an important part to play in understanding and offering and connection. (p. 30)

So we have churches here that have set up in isolation from the local churches in an attempt to create a suitable culture and environment for the members. We will now look at a church that goes further in creating an integrationist model of church that has a prevailing culture appropriate to people with learning disabilities. Eugene Peterson in Jersak (2006), comments on the North American scene which

> honours and celebrates the beautiful, the rich, and the accomplished with spotlighted, centre stage prominence and makes sure that the lepers and Lazarus are kept out of sight (and smell!) backstage. Too much of the church, to its immense shame goes along with the culture. (p. 12)

An integrationist church

What follows is an example of an integrationist model which does not force people with learning disabilities to be other than they are and values them for what they bring in their own right. This demonstrates the Body of Christ as an organism where all parts are fully participative.

Brad Jersak is in church leadership at Fresh Wind Christian Fellowship (British Columbia, Canada) and regards the pillars of his church as 'disabled people, children, prodigals and the poor', through whom he is trying to learn what the Kingdom is about. This is a radical shift as it goes so much further than just including people on the margins to making them central and including people who are well regarded in society as NOT necessarily being the pillars of the church. His book *Kissing the Leper: Seeing Jesus in the Least of These* is likened by Eugene Peterson in his Foreword to a record of 'Jesus sightings' (in an adaptation of birdwatcher parlance). The third section of Jersak's book chronicles encounters with God through people with learning disabilities. Jersak believes that it is possible to see Christ in all people not because they become Christians but because Jesus took on humanity in all its multifacetedness.

Here we introduce three of the people Jersak encounters:

Meghan, a girl with autism; Kathy who is blind in one eye, a wheelchair user and in constant pain, and Pastor Eddie who has Downs syndrome.

He meets Meghan at an art-friendly church called 'Canopy' in Edmonton, where he is their guest speaker. During the worship this young woman went to the front of the church and did a very exuberant and expressive dance. The congregation may have been nonplussed but Brad says he was captivated. Meghan seems to be completely oblivious to what others think and Brad unselfconsciously moves in the same spirit. Brad writes:

> One thing I have learned about autism is that sometimes you can enter the secret world by mimicking the child (or adult) so that is what I proceeded to do. What a sight as suddenly the guest speaker and the little girl repeated the odd anti-choreography together – now twirling, now marching, now thrashing. Scoff, but as King David once said having danced with absolute abandon 'I will become even more undignified than this.' (2 Sam 6.22) (2006, p. 98)

At one point after she has connected with him she walks towards him and grabs his head and pulls it towards her and exclaims enthusiastically: 'You've been to Scotland.' Then she goes into a torrent of 'Hi Scot man, Scot, Scot, Scot, etc.' Unbeknown to her Brad had just returned from Scotland and was struggling with jetlag. She got his attention but then went off on her solo chant again. Finally she started to do a very dramatic and 'threatening' thing pointing at him with her index finger and making throat-slitting gestures! The girl's grandmother jumped up and offered to remove her from the congregation but Brad declined her offer as he believed that God was doing something through this child. Then God told Brad that he was singing about what was happening and he realized that he was singing 'I'm trading my sorrows, I'm trading my shame, I'm laying them down for the joy of the Lord.' As he watched the girl he began to realize that she was cursing the effects of jetlag in his body with the cutting motion and in a matter of minutes he received complete refreshment. He was then able to relay what had happened through Meghan to this church which makes space for the gifts of disabled children.

The second person is Kathy West who is a key member of Brad's church and he describes her as a powerful conduit of God's presence. She has a number of disabilities (as mentioned above). Brad attended a renewal service in the 1990s and Kathy's carer brought her to the front. She joined in where the children were dancing and then she put her hand in Brad's and he asked God to love him through her. On feeling woozy he lay down on the floor. Soon after, 12 hefty bolts like electricity shot through his body and Kathy smirked, dropped his hand and continued with the worship. Brad was perplexed until a few days later his cousin phoned him in distress as she was very unwell. In no time she was being healed which was not his usual experience. Brad believed that he had received the power through Kathy which had acted as a capacitor (a temporary storage for power) until he needed it for his cousin.

There are three men at Brad's church called Tom, Phil and Eddie who all have a gift of bringing suitable scriptures to a situation. Tom does not even read yet he spends hours poring over his Bible and marking verses that seem significant to him. The church has learned to take them all very seriously when they have a scripture to share. On one occasion Brad is about to preach and is feeling troubled that he may have lost the right to speak about the poor as he had just got his first mortgage on a house. He was contemplating asking someone else to speak when Eddie started pointing to a passage before him in his Bible, indicating that he had a word for Brad. The passage was from Jeremiah 29.4–7 where the people are instructed to settle and make homes for themselves with the knowledge that if things go well for them it will go well for the people too. Brad was able to get up and speak without any fear that he had compromised his principles in buying a home for his family. In all these three cases, people with learning disabilities are using their gifts without having to conform to an ableist culture.

Points for Discussion and/or Reflection

1 Does the church exist to meet the needs of the majority or should it aim to accommodate and embrace those on the margins who will not fit the main framework? What might Jesus have to say to us about this tension through Matthew 19.14 'Let the little children come to me, and do not hinder them, for the kingdom of heaven belongs to such as these'?

2 Should we be excited when people with disabilities behave more like those our culture regards as 'normal' or should we be aiming for God to use them as they are so that we 'the so-called normal' can learn more of the nature of God and the values of God's Kingdom?

3 Is there anything that surprises and challenges you in these examples from Fresh Wind Christian Fellowship?

4 How countercultural are the churches you have experienced in terms of power relations?

References

Barnes, C. (1996), 'Theories of Disability and the Origins of the Oppression of Disabled People in Western Society', in Barton, L. (ed) *Disability and Society: Emerging Issues and Insights*, London: Longman, pp. 43–60.

Bryant, A. and Reynolds, G. (2001), *Open to All: A Commitment to a Church accessible to everyone*, Guildford: The Church of England.

Dalpra, C. (2009), *Encounters on the Edge no 44: Hidden Treasures*, Sheffield: Church Army.

Eiesland, N. (1994), *The Disabled God*, Nashville: Abingdon Press.

Fontaine, C. (1995), 'Disability and Illness in the Bible', in Brenner, A., *Feminist Companion to the Bible*, Sheffield: Sheffield Academic Press, pp. 286–300.

Hull, J. (2013), *The Tactile Heart*, London: SCM Press.

Jersak, B. (2006), *Kissing the Leper: Seeing Jesus in the Least of These*, Abbotswood: Fresh Wind Press.

Kelly, B. and McGinley, P. (2000), *Intellectual Disability: The response of the church*, Chorley: Liseux Hall Publications.

Lewis, A. (1983), 'God as Cripple: Disability, personhood and the reign of God', *Pacific Theological Review* 16(11), pp. 13–18.

Majik, P. J. (1994), 'Disability for the religious', *The Disability Rag and Resource* 15, November/December, pp. 24–5.

Newbigin, L. (1989), *The Gospel in a Pluralist Society*, MI: Eerdmanns.

Report (2009), 'Opening the Doors: Ministry with People with Learning Disabilities and People on the Autistic Spectrum', London: General Synod of the Church of England.

Rose, A. (1997), 'Who Causes the Blind to See: disability and quality of religious life', *Disability & Society* 12(3), pp. 395–405.

Shakespeare, T. (1997), 'Cultural Representations of Disabled People: Dustbins for Disavowal', in Barton, L. *Disability Studies, Past, Present and Future*, Leeds: Disability Press.

Swinton, J. (2001), 'A Church for Strangers', *Journal of Religion, Disability and Health* 4(4), pp. 25–63.

Watson, F. (1930), Civilisation and the Cripple, London: Bale.

Webb-Mitchell, B. (1988), *L'Arche: An ethnographic study of persons with disabilities living in a community with non-disabled people*, PhD thesis: University of North Carolina.

Webb-Mitchell, B. (1994), *Unexpected Guests at God's banquet*, New York: Crossroad.

Wilks, J. and Pestell, J. (2003), 'Deaf Perspectives: Challenging Dominant Christian Thought', paper given at London School of Theology 23 November 2003.

World Council of Churches (2003), 'Interim Statement', *A Church of all and for all*, Geneva: WCC.

Yong, A. (2007), *Theology and Down Syndrome*, Texas: Baylor University Press.

Summary

In this chapter the issue of inclusion was foregrounded. Criticisms of the church from the Disability Movement were reviewed and then criticisms from within the church focusing on a frequent tension between the institutional church and the gospel per se. Finally, recent initiatives with doing church for people with learning disabilities were set forth: some parachurch initiatives, including L'Arche, then two examples of niche churches following a separatist model to accommodate to the culture of people with learning disabilities, and finally an integrationist model of church, as a church for all from Brad Jersak in Canada. This last model is a truly radical one that brings the very people society despises, and Jesus calls, to the centre thus refusing to bow the knee to the idolatry of our age, and revere what the world reveres.

7

Conversations with Parents of Disabled Children

In this chapter we will explore how models of disability inform parents who have disabled children (mostly those with intellectual disabilities) and the impact of their underlying belief system in the initial diagnosis.

First a brief note on one of my own experiences. When I was nearly 40 and about to have my first child I was terrified of having a disabled child. The medical world, in the main, was not very supportive of my decision not to have an amniocentesis test. It was interesting that the statistics for the 'risk' of a Downs syndrome child is about the same as the risk of losing the foetus from the amniocentesis, but these statistics were put to me to make the one outcome seem more likely than the other. For example if there is a 1 in 200 chance of a Down syndrome baby it might be expressed like that but that there was only a 0.5 per cent risk from the amniocentesis test, which is the same risk!

On one occasion I went for a scan at 20 weeks and the young doctor looked at my notes and just reiterated that I had opted not to have the amniocentesis. I was so full of frustration for being treated as if I were a bit stupid, that I expressed it to him and he was very open and honest. He told me that women of my age were split about 50/50 in the decision over the test. He also supported my concern that I could lose a perfectly healthy baby by having this procedure. In fact he told me the heart-rending story of friends of his who were in their early forties and were expecting what was likely to be their only child. They finally decided to have the test and after she miscarried the results came back to say all was fine. I am profoundly grateful to him for his candour which cut against the grain of much that I experienced from medical professionals. Of course there are many wonderful people in the medical world but it is the dominant culture of the medical world and some very loud voices within it that is under discussion here. Stefanie and Brian Brock write at length on this from their experience with the birth of their son Adam who has Downs syndrome (Swinton and Brock 2007, pp. 29–43).

I also wish to note that the terrifying prospect of having a Downs syndrome child has now evaporated as I have come to see Downs people very differently. I actually feel deeply ashamed of my previous attitude. I hope that if I ever have a family member with Downs that I will be in a place to offer affirmation and hope to the parents. At almost 40 I had internalized the values of a medical model of disability without awareness of it but I have now done research with people with Downs syndrome and learned to value who they are and what they bring to society. In effect I am now more influenced by a Trinitarian model of disability which embraces all humanity in its rich diversity. I have friends who have adopted children with Downs syndrome to add to their own family. This is a profound move to model to our broken world what the love of Christ can look like in this world. It is what Lesslie Newbigin would call 'a hermeneutic of the kingdom' (Newbigin 1989).

Interviews with Parents of a Disabled Child

In the section that follows I recount the content of four interviews with parents of children with severe disabilities. The names used are fictitious to observe confidentiality. The four individuals are people I have known over some years outside a disability context and the relationship I had with them enabled me to ask for an interview. At the end of each interview I make a comment on the models of disability that the parent has been operating with and in some cases the new model where people move towards a new paradigm. To ensure that the point is strongly made, as I was not controlling what the interviewees said, I made use of the experience of Professor Frances Young (as set out in her books) who had a profoundly disabled son called Arthur, and came to a radical paradigm shift. Moving from a deeply medical and personal tragedy model, she came to see Arthur's life as one to be celebrated for who he was and to recognize that her journey with him had given her access to some deep spiritual realities, and further that he himself had a calling to the church.

Interview material

The interviewees all have an intellectually disabled child, three of the interviews are with mothers and the fourth with a father I know well (these are from four separate families). They come from different geographical locations. Each parent is middle-aged. The subjects are by no means random as I vaguely knew the background and was pleased that I knew four subjects with varying views on their experience. The interview schedule was done over the phone and the four areas that were probed were:

1 First exposure to disability and thoughts and feelings that arose at that time.
2 Initial thoughts and feelings at the diagnosis of your own child. Significant people in the situation who influenced you and ways in which that influence was expressed.
3 Change in perspective over time and if so, in what ways.
4 Any changes on the journey that have been a help.

This was a semi-structured interview where the questions formed a framework from which to explore the area with the freedom to lead off into other areas as the interviewee led. (This is in line with qualitative research methodology.) All the subjects are committed Christians who belong to a church.

Interview 1 – mother (code LSf)

This mother's first experience of disability was when she was about seven and her brother had a friend who had Downs syndrome. While she says she was a bit scared of him she also recalls that they had a lot of fun and laughs when he was around – no suggestion here that he was the butt of the amusement but rather the conduit. So a mixed initial encounter panning out towards the positive.

Her personal experience is complex as she had two children who were later diagnosed with 'special needs'. We will refer to the boy as Simon and the girl as Judy. There were 20 months between them in age and when Simon was five months old he had seizures. Up to that point the only thing they had noted was the possibility that he might be deaf. Simon was taken into hospital and the mother was told that the seizures would cause brain damage. He was in hospital for two weeks and she prayed for the seizures to stop and they did. He has not had any recurrence and is now 29. However, while she was with Simon in hospital a doctor came and was surrounded by medical students. It was clearly not the best 'bedside' environment to break bad news to the mother so she says he kept hedging and moving towards saying something. She sought to put him out of his discomfort and said: 'What are you saying, are you saying he is brain damaged?' To her blunt, unhedged enquiry he simply replied: 'Yes'. The impact was enormous as she had not anticipated this in any way. She was shocked and just gazed out of the window not wanting to allow the realization in. After they took him home in the months and years that unfolded, he did not get speech apart from a few words which ceased when he went to school which apparently is frequently the case. Meanwhile, the older child, Judy was diagnosed with suspected mild Aspergers and they went to London for some light and sound therapy as her hearing was so sensitive that some everyday situations were unbearable. The Auditory Integration Training yielded some improvement. She says that over the years Judy experienced a number of 'touches from God' and felt a growing sense of inner freedom. A well-known and highly respected person in the healing ministry told her that since God had touched one child there was a precedent so she should expect something for Simon too. Judy is now married and has a child and lives abroad whereas Simon lives in a residential home locally with one other man in a flat where his needs are well met. The parents say the story is not over and indeed it is not either for Simon or for them.

In terms of influences on them at that early stage they are well-established members and are now elders in a charismatic church of triumphalistic persuasion – and attend the church of Kenneth Copeland when in the States. Her husband took the view in his initial shock that they served a big God and 'God is bigger than this'. The pastor's wife, a mature and compassionate woman of faith said 'we will face this as it is – and then God'. Her parents-in-law would not talk about it and were very clearly in complete denial and would seek to teach Simon to speak as if he simply lacked tuition. Understandably, this gave rise to some tensions with the parents of Simon.

In terms of the perspective of the interviewee changing she said that the experience had given her empathy and she had started to see that life is more complex than she might have otherwise imagined. She had been able to come alongside others in similar situations and support them. She aims to offer to others what she would have wanted in her own case but did not get. She is grateful to her pastor's wife for lovingly being on the end of the phone often when she would just sob down the phone in distress.

Interview 2 – mother (code GHf)

This mother's first experience of disability, in fact learning disability, was when she was about seven; a shy retiring child, when an older boy (about eleven) at school with Downs syndrome licked her ear. She says she just felt uncomfortable and awkward and not sure how to handle it.

Her son who is profoundly autistic, with no speech and severe epilepsy since puberty, was a premature baby. He was only 2 lbs 9 oz at birth and for a long time he was said to be 'globally delayed' on account of his premature birth. She and her husband were strong Christians from a charismatic background. She believed he could be healed and she says her mother prayed every day. While her church believed in healing miracles they did not express any expectation for her son or support in that way. Her husband was a more complicated influence as he was not able to cope with the reality of this child and eventually divorced his wife (the complex situation with fathers of disabled children is addressed in Chapter 8). When her child was young, he was not able to walk but was given special help and learned to do this. Equally he had a lot of help with speech and language and went to a 'special needs' nursery at the age of three. He was not formally diagnosed with autism until he was 11 when they needed this diagnosis in order to get him into a school for autistic children. A little later he started with seizures which became so severe that under a three-day video telemetry they were able to see that he was having one continuous seizure. Some genetic testing revealed that he had micro-deletion syndrome 2Q 23.1. So it was a gradual realization of how her son was. She holds fast to the significance of the names they gave him and says he was always the child she expected to have. For the sake of anonymity, I cannot reveal his names but simply state that they meant a man of peace and tranquillity, a gift of God, and a mighty warrior. She says he was always a very joyful child who smiled and giggled a lot, also a strong-willed yet gentle boy. At birth he was taken into an incubator and she worried that because she could not feed him but had to express milk to be given in a bottle, he would lack bonding. However, he seems to have managed to bridge the gap in bonding as he was often found with a long hair from his mother wrapped round his thumb which he sucked for comfort. When the nurses removed the hair it was soon seen that he had replaced it.

Two years after the epilepsy began, he started to get drop seizures which are very severe and could knock him out for several hours. Some days he can have up to nine and has had as many as 22 over a weekend and this places great strain on them both. Now he has to wear a special crash helmet and knee pads all the time to protect him if he falls.

She continues to believe he might be healed and says things have improved since a not very well-known person, now a much more high profile and respected 'prophet', told her that there would be improvement with her son; little changes, that would become apparent year on year and this has been her experience.

Interview 3 – father (code GNm)

This father's first experience of any form of disability was with his first child. Ironically it was at the birth of their second child that a nurse noticed something about the behaviour of their then two year old and suggested that all might not be well. She was then diagnosed with classic autism. The positive side of this was that they had gone ahead and had another baby without undue concern. However, after that there was a long gap of seven years during which they processed all the aspects of the new scenario and decided whether to have a third child.

The father (let us call him Nigel) says his initial response was one of complete denial as he had not noticed anything to worry about. Others around him joined in his upbeat assessment of 'Don't worry, it will be all right.' His wife, a medical person, however, had already had some concerns so she accepted the diagnosis more readily and became quite depressed. Her reaction was made more complicated by the fact that she had been prescribed some medication for morning sickness by a medic who had later been struck off the register. She was therefore carrying a lot of fear and guilt. Her low spirit was a problem for her husband as he simply did not know what to do. Because she had just had a second baby it was assumed by one medic that she was suffering from post-natal depression and she even saw on some medical notes that he said she needed to be reassured that her daughter did not have autism as she was suffering from PND. This quite understandably angered her as it was an empty assumption without any foundation whatsoever.

Nigel says her depression led to a lot of confusion for him. It is, of course, very hard to live with a person who is relentlessly upbeat when the other person is depressed Added to this was the fact that being in a charismatic church at the time, some people were quick to leap to the conclusion that God intended to heal the girl. The prospect of healing excited him initially but the lengthy proactive prayer meetings wore him out as they more or less insisted on her healing with bold assertions of confidence and he then had to go home late and be up in the night to attend to this daughter's needs. He says matter of factly that they were surrounded by ignorance, and it had been extremely hard, but being their first child they knew no different. People's desire to pray for healing was well-intentioned but he thinks, on balance, those who offered practical support were more help. He says the professionals in the medical world did what they could which was not very much and then basically said 'Goodbye'. This resulted in them feeling very alone. He adds that trying to go to church with his daughter made life even more complicated as he would often have to take her out into the park. Parents with children who do not have autism sometimes also note the intolerable pressure of trying to keep young children in order during a church service.

In time they heard about a professor in Oslo, Norway, who was working with the ABA (Applied Behavioural Analysis) approach to learning. They set up a home teaching programme and their home became a hub of activity. The approach certainly helped their daughter to get some grasp of language although her language skills continued to be passive/receptive rather than active skills. He says she always liked rhyme and he would make up rhymes for her, for example he would say 'having a laugh in the bath' and she would giggle. He says she always had a very zany sense of humour and seemed to like drama and even enjoyed the sense of circus that her unpredictable behaviour could sometimes cause. He gives the example of a time they were walking along a footpath by a weir and she bent down and removed one of her new shoes and hurled it at the weir. Nigel jumped in trying to rescue the shoe without endangering his own life. Very soon a crowd had gathered and she seemed to like the sense of drama she had unwittingly created. He notes she has no sense of danger so they have to be attentive when near roads as she can just run off. He says she can go into a tea shop, pick up a scone from the plate of an old lady and just crumble it all over the place.

Nigel has learned a lot on his journey with his autistic daughter and he says the focus on healing upsets him now as there are more positive ways in which people can pray: for wisdom and understanding as a parent, and not to become downcast. Also for the strength to be proactive in finding out what resources are available, and to be able to ask for practical help. He says he has learned to stand back and not overreact to the unpredictable things she sometimes does. He says his own reactions sometimes reveal to him his own foolishness and ignorance. He is convinced that through suffering we can come to know Jesus much more deeply. He also feels he has learned a lot about God's love through raising this child.

He says that she is a delight to be with and he has always had a deep connection with her. She is very joyful and one day the staff at her school said she was singing in the toilet and they just stood outside and cried at the beauty of it. One member of staff said that when she comes to work with a problem this girl helps her to get above it with her exuberant presence. Nigel says that a person with a disability is made in the image of God and can be an absolute blessing as they are, and he sees God using her in very creative ways.

He no longer seeks a miraculous healing for her but accepts her as she is and celebrates her life. He is also struck by Matthew 25.36 where Jesus says that he can be found in prison and likewise the hospital – where marginalized people are – so he thinks Jesus wants us to understand that through people like his autistic daughter we can meet Jesus. Nigel's journey seems to be of a type with that of Frances Young (which comes after interview 4) where he has certainly taken on board some of the deeper truths of the Christian faith: a theology of suffering and a countercultural awareness of Christ coming to us in the 'stranger' or those rejected by society.

Interview 4 – mother (code PCf)

This mother's first exposure to disability was when she was young and her brother and sister both had visual impairments. Her brother had to go to a school for the blind even though he had some sight and he was bullied there as his head used to move all the time when he was looking at people as he was trying to focus, so he was called 'Noddy Head'. She says because he had to go away to school Monday to Friday he never really felt part of the family and in the holidays they did not play that well as they did not really know him. She notes that children are very accepting, but with hindsight she says he has had a very narrow life and left school with no qualifications.

The journey with her own son, Jonathan, has been a long one. Initially they noticed that he had a visual impairment which was confirmed by an ophthalmologist who she knew from a mother and baby group. From around one year old she noticed some things that might indicate autism. If she entered the room he did not seem to notice and when she was sitting next to him and said his name he did not turn to her. She wondered if he might have hearing issues too. Also he never pointed and he played in a very repetitive way (called displacement activity as it helps the autistic person cope with the sense of feeling overwhelmed). He would also stare vacantly and not seem to engage much with the world around. Again, another mother with professional training confirmed her suspicion there was an issue. At 18 months he was given the diagnosis of 'social communication disorder' and three months later was diagnosed with autism. He was thought to have Aspergers except that he did not display the obsessive trait common with Aspergers. The parents were told bluntly that he would never learn to communicate meaningfully.

The father of the child was much older and the mother decided that her purpose in life was to 'fix' her child and so she set off on a mission to seek help. She joined a support group and found things online, which was a relatively new resource 20 years ago. They did ABA therapy and through this he learned to speak and also had a good speech therapist who was very affirming of the mother and the progress she was enabling her son to make. They put him on a sugar and gluten free diet and the result was dramatic. Within one week he was speaking and then speaking in sentences. It was such a break-through that at that point she really felt upbeat as if her son was going to get 'fixed'. It was as if she was looking for a cure. She became convinced that his digestive system needed healing and she says that during her time of prayer for this it was as if God healed her of her need for her son to be 'fixed'; she notes God also healed her son's digestive tract. He still has to avoid gluten and sugar or he becomes rather dull and unresponsive. Although he made great strides and is now at university, she says people with autism have brains that are wired differently so from that point of view he will always be autistic – but he can live an independent life now. She says at some point she began to see him as a gift to be enjoyed rather than a problem to be solved.

The speech therapist invited her to join an Alpha course and it was there that she made a recommitment to the Lord and joined a small group. This she sees as providential because her husband had just got into a relationship with another woman and the marriage was unravelling fast. She admits that since her son had become her mission in life her priority had been to the son and not to her husband so he was neglected, plus struggling with his own issues of acceptance that his son was not 'normal' and the sense of disappointment that brought. His parents were elderly so they never really told them the full extent of their child's disabilities and her parents lived abroad and the mother was an alcoholic so again the situation was not conducive to full explanation. It would be interesting to hear the father's version of events but she says she is sure he felt neglected at that time. They were married for ten years in total, but only stayed together for six years after Jonathan was born. She told me that she thought having Jonathan triggered the divorce (Chapter 8 looks at this common issue).

At some point she joined a very triumphalist charismatic church and went on a mission trip to Argentina with them.

There she encountered a lot of emphasis on divine healing and the people there were emphatic that God was going to heal her son. At first she says she felt expectant but in the end when nothing happened she felt very disappointed. She notes that she personally has never felt disappointed in her son.

We can see in this narrative how she started out seeing a disabled person as someone who needed to be fixed or healed in some way. Later she had a major paradigm shift which she attributes to God healing her of her need to have Jonathan 'fixed' and she began to receive him as a gift to be enjoyed and not just a problem to be solved. We note again the struggle of the father and the way in which the marriage eventually fell apart.

While I have not actually interviewed Frances Young regarding her experience with the birth of Arthur, her book *Arthur's Call* gives plenty of information to make the same sort of profile I have done with other people.

Frances Young and Arthur

Frances Young notes her first experience of disability at the diagnosis as being one of shock and bereavement (2014, p. 39). We note again the presence of medical students around the bed at a critically sensitive time of adjustment. Her husband was a highly significant person at this stage as he had had a more severely disabled brother, so was able to make the adjustment relatively easily. Also once they had two further boys her husband took Arthur on as his charge enabling Frances to attend to the other two boys.

Frances seems to have had a thoroughly medical model of disability and even a personal tragedy model. She writes: 'loving my baby I thought I'd accepted him. But at a deeper level acceptance was hampered by the fact that I simply couldn't understand what had happened', 'it was one thing to accept Arthur; it was another to come to terms with the great iceberg of suffering and tragedy that he represented' (2014, pp. 26–7). While acknowledging a sense of tragedy for Arthur she also notes that for her it was the sense of abandonment by God that was the hardest part (p. 28).

However, a close friend commented on the richness of Frances' life and that struck her as a healthy rebuke which enabled her to begin to climb out of the black hole of fears, guilt and self concern that had imprisoned her (p. 29). And in the depth of her despair she sensed a calling from God to go into ordained Christian ministry and later saw her contribution as making a bridge between academic theology and the Christian church. Finally she comes to see that Arthur is at the heart of her calling. Jean Vanier discerned that Arthur had become 'her gateway to God' (p. 123).

The major shift we see in her journey is from a personal tragedy model of disability to what she refers to as 'having privileged access through Arthur to some of the deepest truths of Christianity'. From here she moves from merely being thankful for Arthur to actively rejoicing in him, together with the years of testing and doubts that came with him. She perhaps embraces a Trinitarian model of disability as she sees how significant Arthur is both to her own calling and to the life of the church.

The wilderness is seen as a place of paradox where fear and doubt are met yet also where the love of God is encountered in new ways: 'My fears about the future had disappeared in a new-found trust, hope and serenity, an openness to new possibilities, a readiness to take risks, and let the unexpected happen ... the future was no longer a fearful prospect but an open vista' (p. 45).

Through Arthur she engages with other women on similar journeys and one day takes a woman to visit her son with cerebral palsy, as her previous method of transport had collapsed. This woman had kept his existence a secret at church. Frances has to take Arthur as his legs are in plaster and he is not able to go away with the rest of his family. She concludes, 'So through Arthur we both experienced what the church can be at its best, a community of care and support' (p. 47).

She also sees that 'staying with' rather than 'putting right' (p. 121) is perhaps a deep Christian value and certainly a perception deepened by living with irremovable disability.

Finally it is important to note how the experience with Arthur lays bare her own broken human nature. She recognizes along with all her concerns for him a number of self-orientated passions and concludes: 'I discovered to my shame that I understood how some parents could batter their babies' (p. 146).

From these personal narratives we move on to consider the ethical issue of eugenics and both beginning of life and end of life scenarios.

Beginning and End of Life Issues Relating to Disability

At the current time in the western world there is an implicit belief that if we could stop people with disabilities coming into the world life would be better for all. Yet we see in the interviews that parents of disabled children often do not hold that view.

What follows is largely drawn from the writing of Swinton and Brock in *Theology, Disability and the New Eugenics,* as this is not an in-depth exploration of this topic. I am touching on a number of key points and the reader is encouraged to explore further if interested.

Swinton and Brock consider that science needs the church as our technological knowledge advances at a pace in order to keep our moral bearings. We are alerted to

> a significant and quite profound social contradiction. Major strides are being made towards affirming the full personhood and humanity of people with disabilities and safeguarding their rights, value and personhood in law. At the same time, it is also legally, and for many morally, acceptable that certain forms of disability should be prevented from coming into existence through the use of genetic screening to prevent the birth of disabled children. (2007, p. 6)

Hans Reinders, theological anthropologist and ethicist, asks what kind of message this sends to people with disabilities or indeed to their families? 'On the one hand, we claim we want to accept and welcome people with disabilities, and on the other we say "but everyone would be so much better off if you were not here at all"' (Swinton and Brock 2007, p. 6).

Ethicist Peter Singer promotes 'preference utilitarianism' where people are basically regarded as commodities. Those who cannot make their parents happy are regarded as non-persons and this absolves the parents of any obligation to sustain life. This, in common with all complex questions is not a straightforward question.

Frances Young raises what a true Christian view should be to extending life. She was told by a doctor that in the old days compassionate judgement was often exercised before everything was blown large by the media. I remember my aunt telling me how when her brother was desperately ill after being wounded in the war, witnessing his friend suffer the most unimaginable horrors, and then having cancer himself that in response to his screams a doctor asked for a cup that could be thrown away, poured some substance into it and gave it to the patient who settled down and then peacefully slipped away.

Young cites the case of Dr Arthur who was prosecuted by the Life Organization for assisting an impaired baby to die in peace. She was very moved to hear that Dr Arthur had his Bible in the dock and said:

> I didn't think that 'save life at any price' was an essentially Christian perspective, but rather a legalism demanded by those who daren't risk using their own judgement or trusting anyone else to – an officious meddling with the creator's compassionate arrangements, the panic reaction of those who can't face death, because they've no hope in God.

She contemplates refusing treatment for Arthur the next time he has a chest infection. She asserts that society by treating death as taboo, and by the success of modern medicine, was more cruel than nature, as few severely disabled people used to live beyond their teens. 'Wasn't quality of life more important than quantity?' When she wrote about quality of life at least one reader thought she meant *her* life *their* lives. 'Heaven forbid! I meant the quality of Arthur's life,' she exclaims (2014, p. 14).

John Swinton argues that in this sort of world, the newborn and people with dementia, among others, 'find themselves adrift in an inhospitable world shaped by the values of consumerism'. Sharply he insists:

> we do not view persons as commodities that can be accepted, rejected or exchanged for better models. Persons are fellow creatures whom we should care for and seek ways of being with. In contrast commodities exist to make us happy and as such are expendable and mere matters of choice. (2007, p. 9)

Brent Waters (in Swinton and Brock 2007, p. 9) discerns that in this climate such commodities can be subject to 'quality control' which has become a key component in today's world of procreative liberty.

While it is more often the reality that those who parent children with disabilities do not question their full personhood, we can also see this reality the other way round: when it is our parents who are disabled. Interestingly, Peter Singer's own theoretical work came to be strangely at odds with his lived experience of choosing to care for his mother once she had Alzheimers disease. Previously he had argued for ending the life of such people, yet happily he did not seem so inclined in regard to his own mother.

It is perhaps all too easy for the rational mind to break free from its affective moorings and argue for less than humane policies. We must clearly guard against this rift. The late Swiss psychologist Paul Tournier, in *The Gift of Feeling* (1981), says that when he tried to discuss the topic of divorce with his wife in an abstract way she would always counter 'whose divorce are you talking about?' He was grateful for her constant sense of the person that helped to ground him.

Swinton writes: 'Human beings are persons by virtue of the fact that they are human beings and particular objects of

God's love and salvific intentions' (2007, p. 11). Yet we live in a culture that has learned not to factor in God at all. Swinton suggests that we take seriously the invitation of theologian Walter Brueggemann 'to invite and empower and equip the community to re-imagine the world as though Yahweh were the key and decisive player' (Brueggemann 2000). Swinton cites the wisdom of a person with learning disabilities who stated: 'scientists should find the gene that makes people pick on those who are different, then our lives would be better' (2007, p. 1). We should also note here that disabled people are not frequently asked what they think about eugenics. I have heard some Downs syndrome people say that it is OK having what they have and that we should not stop people with Downs syndrome being born.

Without the accountability that issues from a recognition of God's authority over all things, science can easily stray into practices that are problematic, and especially for some of the most vulnerable members of society.

Genetics and the Christian faith do not need to be at odds. The crucial question is how we engage with the advances in genetic technology, and whether love is central. In such a way it is quite possible, in specific contexts, to encounter God and learn more about the reality of living within the loving orbit of God's presence, power and autonomy.

Hans Reinders says:

> The norms encircling the liberal axis of individual autonomy cannot easily accommodate lives dedicated to the care of perpetually dependent individuals, or admit the intrinsic value of these individuals. (2000, p. 14)

The History of Eugenics

During the 1920s and 30s there was a plethora of publications aimed at enabling Christians to take on board the implications of the theory of evolution. Journals such as *The Methodist Review* and *Religion in Life* forced clergy and laity alike to think at the intersection of evolutionary biology and practical theology (Swinton and Brock 2007, p. 89). Their efforts are important for understanding the fact that eugenics had become an approved project prior to the rise of Nazism and World War Two. The unashamed pursuit of healthy offspring, developing the best of the stock for future generations was sharply challenged once eugenics was put to such horrific use by the Nazis. The revelation of a much darker side to the eugenics project caused the dwindling of public support. It is important, therefore, to note that this debate has been around for a long time and has already taken a number of twists and turns.

At his point it would seem that science and theology were at odds with each other but Walter Doerfler wishes us to see that science and theology are in fact pursuing similar goals: seeking answers to similar questions (Swinton and Brock 2007, p. 118).

Transformation on the Journey with Profound Disability

To close this section I refer to some of the truths uncovered by Christopher de Vinck in *The Power of the Powerless*. He writes about his disabled brother Oliver, reflecting on Oliver's life many years after his death. The abiding impression of his life is the sense of peace that was carried by his presence. In fact he calls their house 'the house of Oliver' as he seems to have been the key participant in this home despite not being able to hold anything, lift his head or even leave his bed. De Vinck says that part of what he learned from Oliver was about the purpose of life. He says that our goal-orientated world can be quite dangerous, as the activism that we value so highly can trip us up into not noticing things that are profound yet need to be noticed and teased out of the mundane and quite ordinary.

Christopher De Vinck also reveals the wisdom gained by his parents who cared for Oliver for 32 years. When he asked his father how he managed such a task for so long he replies that he never in fact cared for him for 32 years but simply one day at a time. Everyday he took on the task of caring for Oliver for one more day and so on until 32 years had passed. Many spiritual guides tell us that this is the way we are intended to live and Jesus underscores this point again and again. 'Therefore do not worry about tomorrow, for tomorrow will worry about itself. Each day has enough trouble of its own' (Matt. 6.34). Oliver de Vinck's mother who was at home with Oliver for many years while her husband was at work, admits that the enforced isolation was very hard for her. Temperamentally she was restless but the charge of caring for Oliver brought her into the embrace of silence and solitude where she claims she learned 'to prepare the way of the Lord'. Powerfully, she states: 'sorrow opened my heart and I "died". I underwent "this death" unaware that it was a trial by fire from which I would rise renewed – more powerfully, more consciously alive' (Swinton and Brock 2007, p. 176).

In conclusion, I invite the reader to listen attentively to the voices of those who have walked with profound disability and experienced what Christians traditionally believe, namely, that death and resurrection are linked and when we are called to die to ourselves it is for the purpose of rising to newness of life.

Points for Discussion and/or Reflection

1 What either shocked or impressed you most in the five testimonies (including that of Frances Young)?
2 Which of the five subjects do you most identify with and why? If none, also why?
3 What is your response to the new eugenics? Did anything in this section challenge you personally?

References

Brueggemann, W. (2000), *Deep Memory, Exuberant Hope, Contested Truth in a Post-Christian World*, Minneapolis: Fortress Press.
De Vinck, C. (1988), *The Power of the Powerless*, New York: Doubleday.

Newbigin, L. (1989), *The Gospel in a Pluralist Society*, MI: Eerdmanns.

Reinders, H. S. (2000), 'The meaning of life' in liberal society, in *Meaningful care: A multidisciplinary approach to the meaning of care for people with mental retardation*, Dordrecht: Kluwer, pp. 65–84.

Swinton, J. and Brock, B. (2007), *Theology, Disability and the New Genetics*, London: T&T Clark.

Tournier, P. (1981), *The Gift of Feeling*, London: SPCK.

Young, F. (2014), *Arthur's Call*, London: SPCK.

Summary

In this chapter we explored the personal world of a number of people who have had a child with profound learning disabilities. Three mothers and one father were interviewed and the questions probed the internal framework with which they understood disability and shifts that may later have occurred. Alongside the four interviews stands the experience of theologian Frances Young recorded in her book *Arthur's Call* concerning her developing understanding of the experience of having a profoundly disabled child. This is useful as Frances Young probably undergoes a greater paradigm shift than any of my interviewees, but then she reflected over many years and as a working theologian and priest. Echoes of her testimony are heard in some of the other interviews notably in Nigel's who recognizes the deepening of his faith as he struggles to come to terms with his disabled daughter and meets Jesus more in the teeth of his own suffering. A movement towards celebrating the life of the person is seen in several of the interviews away from simply regarding the person as a case to be fixed. Beginning and end of life issues were explored in relation to disability. The history of eugenics is set out and the implications of the new eugenics for the most vulnerable in society. The countercultural challenge of engaging with profound disability and the spiritual transformations that this can lead to are acknowledged.

8

Pastoral Concerns for
Support of Families

Carry each other's burdens, and in this way you will fulfil
the law of Christ. (Gal. 6.2)

This final chapter leads to the critical question of how to
offer meaningful pastoral support to families who live with
impairments of many kinds. Some examples are given from the
context of Costa Rica. A prophetic challenge is raised from the
parable of the great banquet (Luke 14.15–24) examining how
best to bear one another's burdens among this constituency
and this is linked to initiatives practised by this author. This
will return us to the point that Christianity is about interdependence and community however unfashionable that may be
in today's culture.

In this final chapter we look at pastoral ways in which we can
both empathetically support and practically bear one another's
burdens. There are a number of areas to be addressed here. In
my own situation when my son was too unwell for school for
a great number of years, I learned the importance of a bit of
fun and light relief when on such a long and arduous journey.
At this time I had a lot of support: a very caring and understanding husband, a host of supportive friends, good financial
undergirding and the use of a flat on the Dorset coast. I became
aware of women around me with far less support than me and
felt I wanted to do something to give them a bit of a lift.

Supporting Mothers and Other Women

I read the parable of the great banquet which is a tricky one in our western context as we say 'there is no such thing as a free lunch' and in the main people are suspicious of such things. Two things I noted in the parable that could be translated into any cultural context were that the gift was non-reciprocal and that the objects of the giver were people who society, in the main, ignored and pushed to the margins.

I therefore decided to get a number of women together at my home and have what came to be known as foodie/movie evenings. I would choose a suitable DVD (nothing too emotionally demanding) and ideally set somewhere beautiful, also known for its good food, say Tuscany or Provence. In summer we would have Prosecco in beaten pewter flutes and in winter mulled wine in glass mugs round the wood burner. I would prepare some finger food to eat during the movie and sometimes guests made wonderful offerings of food too. So from doing it all myself we moved to a more collaborative evening in which I was merely the facilitator. Mostly we were around six at a time and in private I called them my 'beleagured mums' even though some were not necessarily mothers at all but under pressure from some other area in life. Mostly they were people with a long-term issue, such as a disabled child, many were single parents and some were people struggling to stay in challenging marriages that were not abusive, difficult for some other reason, but the couple loved each other and wanted to stay together for the sake of each other as well as for the children. This latter situation constitutes another long journey that needs support and nurture to survive in. Equally we had people who were single with no siblings or parents and who had emotionally demanding jobs working in such roles as hospital chaplain. Some of the people I invited happened to be Christians but in the main they were a mix of local people as there was emphatically no agenda! For women with a profoundly disabled family member, not in institutional care, some form of provision for them will need to be offered, to enable them to come to such an evening.

Of course men need this sort of support too but sometimes we just have to do the little thing that God puts on our heart and let others do other things that are more suited to their life experience and gifts. Only together with every member of the body working together can we ever hope to meet all the many needs that life creates. We will look next at some of the support that men might benefit from, especially in this context of people with a disabled family member.

Before moving on I would like to issue a challenge to women who enjoy entertaining and hospitality and may have wonderful homes and a special environment to share with others. Instead of always inviting friends to dinner who can return the invitation, why not sometimes have an evening for a handful of women who have a disabled child and could do with a bit of pampering. Consider the parable in Luke 14.15–24, and why not consider if you know any disabled people who might like to come (this includes people with mental health issues). My husband is friendly with two men in the next street. They are close friends of each other; one has mental health issues and the other cerebral palsy and learning disabilities. The latter walks with crutches and in the summer it is easier for him to access our home in the back garden so we do a barbecue for them each summer. These are little things but my challenge is to widen our horizons so that we include people not usually much considered in society or indeed often in the church either.

Supporting Fathers

Fathers with a disabled child first came on my radar when I was talking about this book to a friend, Brenda Darke, who works in Costa Rica and teaches on disability and the church all over Latin America. She told me that they had learned the need to support the man first or he would go under and the marriage would break down. In her own case it had often been too late once they had thought about the father's needs. In her context she believed that the macho culture in Latin America would cause additional issues for the father as the existence of a disabled child might challenge his self-esteem in particular ways. Brenda told me of one particular couple who had managed to stay together long term and she believed they had kept their faith though not attending a church as far as she knew. She said the woman only had Sunday as a day off from work and the man who cared for the child at home most of the time played football on Sundays for exercise and relaxation. This might also flag the need for church leaders to discern other ways of supporting people for whom the expectation to attend Sunday church services might represent yet another hurdle in their already overstretched lives.

Divorce rates are higher among couples who have a disabled child. I suspect this is because it causes a sifting and if the marriage was basically self-serving (which all marriages probably are to some degree) and there is not a strong love at the core, it will not hold once the attractions of the relationship disappear. Another reason is pointed out by Heather Featherstone her book *A Difference in the Family*. When something goes wrong in the marriage, it is natural to begin to question the validity of the marriage itself. (This is especially toxic where the marriage had been opposed by a close family member or more than one.) I dare say the reverse is true, that when a couple give birth to the child of their dreams that it will tend to reinforce the rightness of the marriage.

The Fatherhood Institute (The UK's think-and-do-tank for fathers)

The Fatherhood Institute exists to provoke debate and to research fathers in society generally, and some of their findings are of interest here.

Herbert and Carpenter (1994) note that fathers may experience the diagnosis of a disabled child in an even more intense way than the mothers and therefore the process of adjustment can be drawn out and turbulent (Harrison et al. 2007; Hornby 1992). In a small-scale study Herbert and Carpenter showed the reactions to the birth as being different among mothers and fathers, yet the fathers often assuming their response was the same as the mothers (Rendell 1997). In the last chapter we saw in interview 3 with Nigel that his reaction was radically different from his wife's and he found that disconcerting, as he was robustly in denial. People are always individuals and thus react very differently from one another. Some women say they find stoicism reassuring, while others see 'a silent fortitude as an alarming indication of denial or indifference' (Brown 1976, p. 61). This lack of connection between the couple can lead to a deep resentment on the part of the person who is in touch with their pain. One mother comments: 'In my grief and frustration I grew to hate my silent husband, never realizing that he was suffering too. His dreams were broken. It was his child too – and his unhappy marriage' (p. 61).

A Victorian model of fatherhood was seen to produce problems as where the father believed it was his duty to be strong for his wife, this mitigated against honesty and vulnerability over his true feelings. Herbert and Carpenter note 'their sense of failure where this proves difficult or impossible can be serious' (1994). They found that some fathers dealt with the situation through increased use of alcohol and working longer hours to avoid their pain. One study found that fathers were influenced by the response of their own parents, so accepting grandparents increased the father's own capacity to accept (Waisbren 1980).

There was also a social class variable as fathers from lower income families tended to be affected more adversely by the birth of a disabled child and spent less time with the child in contrast to higher income and better educated families where more time was spent with the child (Lamb and Laumann-Billings 1997). In addition, mothers talked about the stresses of daily living while fathers reported loss of satisfaction with family life.

Fathers who were not able to adjust frequently suffered from depression. The concern here is that professionals were less likely to pick up on this with the father than with the mother. While some people may be looking to the father for support at a time when he is in turmoil, Carpenter notes 'the needs of the father, among them for him to be nurtured himself, often go unrecognized by professionals' (2005, p. 192). A substantial body of research shows that the fathers were often not included and felt ignored, by health-care and education professionals. Further they were depicted in reports as 'the invisible parent' (Ballard 1994); 'the peripheral parent' (Herbert and Carpenter 1994); and 'hard to reach' (McConkey 1994). It may well be that the authorities were still operating out of an outdated (Victorian) view of fatherhood where the father is expected to be distant but strong in a crisis and for this reason some fathers found it hard to assert their right to involvement. In 2007, The Foundation for People with Learning Disabilities noted an improvement in the inclusion of some fathers. A report from New Zealand poignantly called 'Perilous Passage' explores the father's feelings at this time of great turmoil and distress.

For those who struggle to adjust, a support group of other fathers in a similar situation was found to be beneficial. However, as Heather Featherstone noted, some men said that talking could not change anything. This is also a common issue in counselling where the person believes that only a change in their circumstances can provide any relief, whereas a paradigm shift is frequently very beneficial but not the 'fix' that the person would prefer. Meeting with others who are further along the road may be helpful, as it reveals that progress is possible. A young social worker says of a group he ran briefly 'the fathers came once or twice at the most. They said the disabled child had ruined their life and left' (Featherstone 1980, p. 129). Featherstone notes: 'For a man who finds it difficult to face the full extent of the tragedy, an encounter with other men facing similar problems can bring real help' (p. 128). There were some fathers who made a good adjustment and spoke of personal growth as a result (Meyer 1995).

The 'Recognizing Fathers' project has highlighted the need for fatherhood to be given status and equality and especially for fathers of disabled children to be offered respect and support. In the twenty-first century many fathers of children with 'special needs' are playing a crucial role balancing work and home life along with their partners. So from supporting the father we need to move on to look at the need to support the marriage.

High Risk of Divorce: Myth and Fact

There has been a lot of alarmist talk around this subject and the last thing a person who has just given birth to a child with impairments wants to hear is that they are now more likely to divorce. They are reeling from the first shock and do not need this sort of worry to be lurking on top of all the other fears that are taking hold.

Some of the more alarming figures have been tested and found to be way too high. Apparently, the figure of 80 per cent of people with an autistic child ending up divorcing is a very common statistic. Responsible researchers have examined this claim further and found it to be greatly exaggerated. The National Autistic Society looked into this 'urban legend' (apparently an oft quoted statistic on American celebrity and talk shows). Naseef and Freedman show that having an autistic child increases the strain between parents, but this is in the context of a 40–50 per cent divorce rate in the regular population. An article published in 2013 by The Autistic Society notes that right back in 1951, Kramer commented on the surprisingly low incidence of divorce among families he saw who had an autistic child. Data from the national survey indicated that 64 per cent of children with autism live with both parents. It is important to shed light on this topic as Alysia Abbott points out in *Psychology Today* (July 2013) that in interviews with parents she frequently encountered this statistic as received wisdom in society. The reality is that as for all parents, a family needs work and commitment and pulling together is a choice that will strengthen the marriage. It is crucial to disseminate hope to couples without fudging the reality of life's struggles.

Calleen Petersen discovered a research study published by the National Institute of Health which noted that many studies failed to take a long-term view of the marriage and just concentrated on the divorce rate in the first few years. In considering the lifetime of the marriage the significant variable was not disability but family size. The larger the family the more likely divorce was except where there was a disabled child and then the more siblings there were the less likely divorce was – the article surmised that this was due to the extra support available.

In many churches in the twenty-first century, there are now marriage courses to help couples strengthen their marriages. Marriage counsellors are aware of the impact of a particular reaction from one party on the other, sometimes known as 'the mobile effect'. Again Featherstone notes: 'Her optimism may have reinforced his pessimism and vice versa'. Each person counterbalances the other; each unconsciously adjusts his or her position to preserve a certain equilibrium. During a nice dinner eaten at a table for just the two a private discussion will follow some input from a talk. In acknowledging the extra strain that marriages are under where a disabled child is a factor, might it not be wise to offer such a resource to enable these couples to have a relaxing evening together over a meal where discussion can help them flag any problems that might be brewing. Since the existence of a disabled child also greatly increases the financial burden in a family such couples may not have sufficient extra money to go out for romantic meals and such a provision might in itself strengthen the relationship.

Points for Discussion and/or Reflection

1 Did you learn anything new about the support needs of people with a disabled child?
2 Is there something you could imagine doing to be a support in this context?

References

Abbott, A. (2013), 'Love in the time of autism', *Psychology Today.*

Ballard, K. (1994), *Disability, Family, Whanau and Society*, Palmerston North, New Zealand: Dunmore Press.

Brown, H. (1976), *Yesterday's Child*, New York: M. Evans.

Carpenter, B. (2005), 'Early Childhood Intervention: Possibilities and prospects for professional families and children', *British Journal of Special Education*, vol. 32(4).

Featherstone, H. (1980), *A Difference in the Family*. London: Penguin Books.

Harrison, J., Henderson M. and Leonard, R. (2007), *Different Dads: Fathers' Stories of Parenting Disabled Children*, London: Jessica Kingsley.

Herbert, E. and Carpenter, B. (1994), 'Fathers – the secondary partners; professional perceptions and fathers' reflections', *Children & Society*, 8(1), pp. 31–41.

Hornby, G. (1992), 'A review of fathers' accounts of their experience of parenting children with disabilities', *Disability, Handicap & Society*, 7(4), pp. 363–74.

Lamb, M. E. and Laumann-Billings, L. A. (1997), 'Fathers of children with special needs', in *The Role of the Father in Child Development* (3rd edn), New York: John Wiley & Sons.

McConkey, R. (1994), 'Early intervention: planning futures, shaping years', *Mental Handicap Research*, 7(1), pp. 4–15.

Meyer, D. (1995), *Uncommon fathers: Reflections on Raising a Child with a Disability*, Bethesda, MD: Woodbine House.

Naseef, R. and Freedman, A. (2012), 'A diagnosis of autism is not a prognosis of divorce', *Autism Advocate*, Fall: Google Scholar, pp. 9–12.

Petersen, C. (2018), Wisconsin Longitudinal study. National institute of Health.

Rendell, D. (1997), 'Fatherhood and learning disabilities: a personal account of reaction and resolution', *Journal of Learning Disabilities for Nursing Health and Social Care*, 1(2), pp. 77–83.

Waisbren, S. (1980), 'Parents' reactions to the birth of a developmentally disabled child', *American Journal of Mental Deficiency*, 84, pp. 345–51.

Summary

In this chapter we took up some of the themes that came to light in some of the interviews, and also in much of the literature, namely, the need to support mothers and fathers individually and as marriage partners together under the potential trauma and inevitable strain of having a profoundly disabled child. The popular view that there was an 80% risk of divorce when an autistic child is born into the family was examined, and although this was found to be alarmist, certain increased risks were noted. The challenge for support was seen as pressing, and some concrete ways that this could be worked out were suggested.

Conclusion

As we have seen disability provides a lens through which we can more honestly see ourselves as limited human beings, made in the image of a relational God; and a lens through which we can better understand the values of the upside-down kingdom of Jesus Christ. The Kingdom is based on not considering ourselves more highly than others, and indeed on preferring the interests of the other above our own. Further, from here we can embrace what Sally McFague calls 'the scandal of Christianity', namely, that the teachings of Jesus demand that we engage lovingly with those on the margins of society.

This work also challenges the assumption that disabled people should be marginal rather than occupying the central place of our concerns and endeavours. As those who have been exiled to the margins are drawn to the centre, the centre becomes better informed and in the sense that it is an elitist/ exclusivist point of reference it becomes demolished. We all move on to a level playing field where together we are held in the circle of embrace, every member equally called to image Christ. This kind of community becomes a truly sacred place for it is where the Trinitarian God dwells, extending the warm hospitality of those who welcome the stranger in the sure knowledge that as we reach out to others in love we ourselves will be transformed. There is a circular dynamic here; we all win as transformation is not what 'they' need but what God wishes to gift to 'us' – a greater way of being. The hierarchical dynamics of power become flattened. As Vanier pointed out as we embrace the stranger within us, perhaps, what Jung would call 'the shadow side', we are enabled to embrace the stranger without. We need to draw away from a popular perspective that people are either wholly good or totally evil, for we are all a mix of both and where we fail to recognize our own shadows we tend to project them on to others (possibly one reason why Christians are called to love their enemies). We do well to remember the Christian tradition that teaches that we may encounter God or an angel in the stranger, thus ensuring that our attitude is one of the utmost respect. Returning to the image of the circle of embrace, this fulfils an age-long impulse in Christianity towards community and hospitality based on reverence for the other.

Moving away from an individualistic and fiercely independent society has been seen to be pivotal in the support of families with disabled members. We have seen how the Industrial Revolution which split work from home was not generally a good thing either for women or for disabled people. Women, who are often the primary carers for disabled family members, are forced out of the workforce and isolated at home. This rift also causes the same isolation to disabled people who were previously valued members of the community. Nevertheless the testimony of Oliver's mother in Chapter 7 speaks powerfully of the fruitfulness that can come from such a painful death to the ego, while the true self yields to Christ. Here we see an example of how disability challenges our demand for control and a life of ease. The problem is systemic and Jesus himself challenged the system and paid the ultimate price for doing so. While we have noted that there is some controversy within the Disability Movement over the healing miracles, yet the fact is that God wills wholeness and shalom and that will come most fully through society being transformed and all barriers, physical, intellectual and attitudinal being abolished.

So what recommendations does this work suggest for us as the church?

Educational Tasks

To flag that:

- Disability has not always been a separate category in society and that there are many different way of thinking about disability according to the models we internalize. A personal tragedy narrative is just one story we can tell about disability but there are other more life-affirming options. The moral meaning of disability has shifted across time and across cultures. There is no one self-evident, universal meaning of disability.
- All people are made in the image of God, irrespective of disability, gender, etc.
- All people are made to be in relationship with God even if they lack speech, for God is beyond words and desires to be in relationship with all his children.
- All embodied beings live within limits.
- The concept of normality is not a helpful or neutral concept. It is a social construction that excludes whereas the image of God is inclusive and not an idealized or romanticized projection.
- Suffering is part of the human condition and not necessarily indicative of sin or a curse. The theology of suffering is a bona fide aspect of our faith, as is the fact that God works in all things for his good purposes.
- When we have to die to something we love we need to be assured that in death there is the seed of resurrection life and something new will come to birth in its place.
- Challenging the status quo is not an optional aspect of the call to follow Jesus.
- The values of our age lead us to seek control and a life of comfort, and disability challenges those values. Disability can cause us to engage with the upside-down values of the Kingdom and to grow in maturity and deep faith. Resurrection life flows from the cross.
- The Body of Christ as a welcoming and loving community is central to a demonstration of the gospel. Also embracing the

'stranger' in our midst is a core Christian practice of hospitality from ancient tradition.
- That people with disabilities are part of the Body of Christ as they are, on the same basis of mutuality as all others members; both giving and receiving.

Spiritual/Theological Frameworks

- Teaching a more contemplative approach to life: living in the present moment and receiving God's love and grace for each day and discerning where God is in the journey, would lend more support than any kind of quick fix theology which might set the individual at odds with their situation and possibly trip them up into feeling cheated by God.
- An emphasis that 'in all things God works for the good of those who love him, who have been called according to his purposes' (Rom. 8.28). Also that God is refining us so that we can reflect his glory in our lives more easily.
- That we are not called to walk our situation alone but to receive the support of the Christian community to which we belong.
- That 'staying with' rather than 'putting right' is a value to be strengthened.
- Providing preparation for preaching on texts that foreground disability or use metaphors of disability in a problematic way.
- Teaching hermeneutics to the congregation as standard (see Further Reading).
- Providing prayer spaces where people, including those with profound disabilitites can experience the presence of God, as did the contemplatives such as Teresa of Avila and Francis of Assisi and others.

Support Tasks

As we saw in Chapters 7 and 8 the reality of people with disabilities puts a heavy burden on families and indeed on marriages. It is important that the Body of Christ finds ways in which to offer support, both practically and in terms of morale.

Practically speaking this might involve:

- A pampering evening with nice food and maybe an uplifting film for women who are in a tough place. This is an opportunity to offer the sort of generous hospitality mentioned in Luke 14.15–24 which will not be reciprocated. This is one of many ways in which we can embrace a countercultural ethic: giving for no selfish gain.
- For fathers a support group to share with other men who have been faced with the same huge challenge. Perhaps a course that looks at the ways in which men and women may respond differently to the birth of a disabled child and the impact of that on the marriage.
- For couples a type of marriage course with additional specialized content for those managing the stresses and financial strain of having a disabled child.
- Perhaps the provision of some kind of retreat/respite for the couple.
- Although this has not been mentioned earlier in the text I do know people from a local church who run a holiday club for people with disabilities and their families. It is a highly labour-intensive project and devours a lot of resources and for that reason alone it is an inspiring example of countercultural praxis.

Further Reading

Rogers, A. P. (2016), *Congregational Hermeneutics*, Abingdon: Taylor & Francis.

Glossary

Anachronistic Belonging to a period other than the one under discussion.

Anthropology The scientific study of cultures and human societies and their development.

Apophatic theology Approaching God by means of speaking only what may not be said about God.

Cataphatic theology The opposite of apophatic. The knowledge of God explored only through positive statements.

Classical theism In which God is seen as the absolute metaphysical ultimate being.

Conundrum A confusing and difficult problem or question.

Deism An ultimate creator who does not intervene in the world he has created.

Diachronic resurrection identity An attempt to explain what it is that makes an entity identical with an entity existing at another time.

Egocentric Orientated towards the self.

Emergent In the process of becoming prominent.

Epiphany A moment of sudden and great revelation.

Epistemology The theory of knowledge and focuses on what is known to be true.

Escahatology Theology concerned with the life to come.

Essentialist A belief that things can be defined by a set of characteristics which make them what they are.

Eugenics Controlled breeding to improve the quality of the human population.

Gatekeepers Those who control access to something.

Generalizable Able to be made more widely or generally applicable.

Gnostic A belief that matter is evil and souls are trapped in the body, so mystical knowledge is valued to transcend the body.

Hegemonic Ruling in a political context.

Homiletics The study of how to deliver a religious message.

Hylemorphic anthropology A way of looking at the relationship between the body and soul.

Imago Dei That human beings are created in the image of God.

Impassable That God is not subject to pain, suffering or uncontrolled emotions.

Incarnational A living being embodying the divine spirit.

Intellectual access Ensuring that written and spoken matter is not made obscure through the use of complex words or abstract language and concepts.

Medieval synthesis The blending of Greek thought with Christianity initiated by Thomas Aquinas who was influenced by Aristotle, and Augustine by Plato.

Minjung theology A 'peoples' theology specific to the Korean context emerging from South Korea's struggle for social justice in the 1970s.

Missio Dei The idea that God is the one who sends to fulfil God's own mission to the world.

Mujerista theology A feminist liberation theology for Latinas in the United States.

Ontological A branch of metaphysics dealing with the nature of being.

Oralism movement The education of deaf students through speech: lip reading and mimicking the mouth shapes and breathing patterns of speech. It became popular in the US from the 1860s and was the major interest of Alexander Bell who invented the telephone.

Othering To treat another person as intrinsically different from and alien to oneself.

Pedagogue A rather strict teacher.

Phenomenology The philosophical study of observed unusual people or events as they appear without any further study or explanation.

Philanthropy A desire to promote the welfare of others, especially through generous donations of money to good causes.

Pneumatological Relating to the work of the Holy Spirit.

Preference utilitarianism Values actions that fulfil the maximum amount of personal interest.

Salvific Leading to salvation.

Sociocentric Orientated towards one's own social group.

Talmud A commentary on the Torah.

Theodicy An attempt to vindicate divine providence with the realization of evil and suffering in the world.

Theory of accommodation The theory that while God is unknowable and unreachable that God nevertheless, is able and desires to make himself known to all humankind.

Thomist Hylemorphism States that there is a immaterial soul and material body, but the soul is not just stuck in the body as Plato thought. Rather the immaterial soul and the material body are intimately connected and, though it might be an oversimplification to say it this way, the soul shapes, in a sense, the form of the body.

Universalistic A view that God intends for all to be saved.

Womanist A form of feminism especially for women of colour.

Xenophobia Prejudice and dislike of people from other countries.

Index of Names and Subjects